A

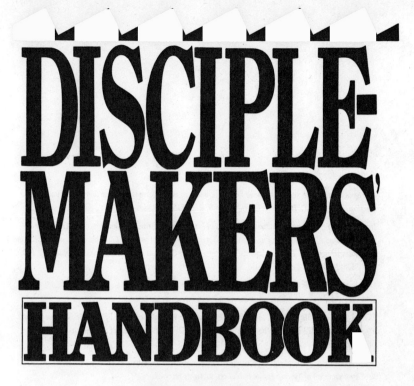

DISCIPLE-MAKERS' HANDBOOK

Alice Fryling, editor
with contributions from
J. Michael Basler
Phyllis Le Peau
Meri MacLeod

INTERVARSITY PRESS
DOWNERS GROVE, ILLINOIS 60515

InterVarsity Press is the book-publishing division of Inter-Varsity Christian Fellowship, a student movement active on campus at hundreds of universities, colleges and schools of nursing. For information about local and regional activities, write Public Relations Dept., InterVarsity Christian Fellowship, 6400 Schroeder Rd., P.O. Box 7895, Madison, WI 53707-7895.

Distributed in Canada through InterVarsity Press, 860 Denison St., Unit 3, Markham, Ontario L3R 4H1, Canada.

"The A-B-C Plan of Bible Study" taken from "How to Take Hold of the Bible," by Don Fields in the January 1970 HIS, the official student publication of InterVarsity Christian Fellowship of the USA and used by permission.

"Checklist for Discovering Learning Channels" taken from How to Help a Friend by Paul Welter © 1978, used by permission of Tyndale House Publishers, all rights reserved.

"A Four-Week Plan for Developing Evangelism Skills" taken from A 30-Day Evangelism Plan, by Len Andyshak © 1986 by InterVarsity Christian Fellowship of the USA and used by permission of InterVarsity Press, P.O. Box 1400, Downers Grove, IL 60515.

All Scripture quotations, unless otherwise indicated, are from the Holy Bible, New International Version. Copyright © 1973, 1978, International Bible Society. Used by permission of Zondervan Bible Publishers.

ISBN 0-8308-1266-0
Printed in the United States of America ∞

Library of Congress Cataloging-in-Publication Data
The Disciplemakers' handbook : helping people grow in Christ / edited
  by Alice Fryling.
    p. cm.
  Includes bibliographical references.
  ISBN 0-8308-1266-0
  1. Discipling (Christianity)   I. Fryling, Alice.   II. Title:
Disciplemakers' handbook.
BV4520.D57   1989
248.4—dc20   89-36648
                                                CIP

16	15	14	13	12	11	10	9	8	7	6	5	4	3	2	1
99	98	97	96	95	94	93	92	91	90	89					

Preface

This book is written in the first person, but I want to tell you a secret: behind every *I* stand four people, four who are eager to help you become an effective disciplemaker.

Working on this manuscript has been a surprise as well as a challenge for me. When InterVarsity Press approached me about editing a book on how to disciple young Christians, my first response was that they were barking up the wrong tree. I have never been very successful using one method for teaching faith in Jesus. While I admire the ability of some to define the discipleship process, I have never been able to decide on just one technique for myself. And besides, I wasn't sure I wanted to add to the multitude of discipleship programs on the market today. No, I decided, I was not the one to work on this book.

But the idea would not let go of me. Perhaps I could write a book that someone like me would want to read! And working with several other writers, as they were suggesting, would reduce the risk of a one-method or one-style approach.

Perhaps we could write not about *methods,* but about *relationships.* Perhaps we could talk not about *formulas,* but about *growth* and *ideas.* Perhaps. . . .

The next thing I knew I was meeting with three other writers, Mike Basler, Phyllis Le Peau and Meri MacLeod. We brainstormed ideas about how to define a disciplemaker. Since we hardly knew each other before we started writing together, we needed to talk a lot about disciplemaking. Much to my delight, I found that we were thinking along the same lines.

We all agreed that the essence of Christian discipleship is *relationship.*

Jesus extended the invitation "Come to *me*" (Mt 11:28). He did not invite people to adopt a certain philosophy, or even to join a certain group, but to come into a relationship with him. His instructions to his first disciples were to "go and make disciples of all nations" (Mt 28:19). Later, God's instructions to the early church were reflected in Paul's words to Timothy, "The things you have heard me say in the presence of many witnesses entrust to reliable men who will also be qualified to teach others" (2 Tim 2:2).

Disciplemaking, then, is at the heart of the message of the gospel.

The concept of disciplemaking may be better understood today as mentoring. A mentor, in a spiritual sense, is sometimes called a spiritual director. According to Robert E. Webber, author of *The Majestic Tapestry,* the idea of spiritual directorship is coming back into vogue. He notes that the office of spiritual director is rooted in the early church. The monastic monks saw the need for individual direction and instruction. They concluded from the teaching of the New Testament and from the example of Paul and Timothy that we are members of the body of Christ and that we need each other to provide direction for spiritual growth.

Webber goes on to say:

The office of a spiritual director is not an actual church office but a function of the body. A mature Christian assumes responsibility toward one or more other Christians and guides them through regular counsel into a disciplined growth in Christ. The ultimate task of a spiritual director is to help younger Christians find the will of God. In the process, the director may help the person develop disciplined habits of prayer and spiritual reading, may listen to the confession of sins, and may encourage and counsel the growing Christian in many areas of life.[1]

We may adopt this as our definition of disciplemaking.

We are part of a process. We are Christians today because through the centuries men and women have responded obediently to these words in Scripture. This book is an attempt to help people in our day to continue to respond in obedience, to continue to be part of God's intention to bring all nations to himself.

The first half of this book defines and describes the disciplemaking process. Each chapter is followed by a section of questions, entitled "Putting It All Together," to be used by individuals or by small groups. If you are a new disciplemaker, this section will help you visualize the potential in disciplemaking. If you are a veteran disciplemaker, perhaps this section will sharpen your vision in areas where your disciplemaking skills need to grow and develop. As we wrote this book we have certainly challenged each other in this way.

In the second half of the book, each chapter discusses a skill which is essential to disciplemaking—how to be a friend, how to model the Christian life, how to establish a disciplemaking relationship, how to help people change, how to use Scripture in disciplemaking, how to help a friend who hurts and how to help a friend share the faith.

At the end of each chapter, in addition to the discussion questions, you will find specific resources to help you implement the ideas in the chapter.

Effective learning takes place when we work with new ideas to make them fully a part of our own thinking and acting. This book is designed not just to give you information on how to be a disciplemaker, but also to help you integrate these new ideas into your daily relationships. If you follow the exercises after each chapter, you will begin to develop skills necessary for being an effective disciplemaker. If you work through this book with another person—or better still, a small group—you will gain the most from it. Our intention in writing is not just that you will learn new things *about* discipleship, but that you will actually become a disciplemaker.

On a more personal note, one of my concerns is that we not come across as super-people. This is a risk in writing any book, but when there are four authors, the risk is magnified four times. We are not super-people. We are all disciplemakers, but we are ordinary people. Two of us are homemakers and two of us are campus staff workers with InterVarsity Christian Fellowship. We all love students and we all have been actively involved with IVCF chapters for many years. Our experiences in disciplemaking have been enhanced by our student relationships but by no means limited to them. What we love the most is to see our friends, students and others, learn to love Jesus more.

We have all also been on the receiving end of God's love to his people through his people. We are not just ministers of the gospel; we have all been ministered to by others. Just today I received a phone call from a new friend who had heard pain in my voice the day we met (she was right) and she called to reach out and touch my life with the love of Jesus. (She did.) I could name dozens of people who have influenced me in many of the same ways I hope to influence others.

Another concern I have is that those who read this book not feel obliged to implement every idea we have suggested. To do this would be contrary to Scripture. We are not all gifted to do everything. "Just as each of us has one body with many members, and these members do not all have the same function, so in Christ we who are many form one body, and each member belongs to all the others. We have different gifts, according to the grace given us" (Rom 12:4-6). As you read, look for what God is saying to you personally. Begin to act according to the good gifts he has given to you. Don't make the mistake of thinking that God expects all things from all people.

The other day I received a piece of mail from a local department store. The envelope read, "Just for you, our special customer." But it was addressed to Current Resident. So much for being personal!

God is not like that. He knows that we are unique and treats us as such. He has equipped each one of us for a special job. You may find some of what you need to do that job in the skills of disciplemaking discussed in this book. Whatever your work, God bless you as you seek to discern his specific will for you.

One final word about pronouns. I've already told you that every _I_ in this book means _we_. All the stories in this book are based on real-life happenings. But all the names have been changed, and whether the _I_ or the main character is a he or a she is up to you to decide!

Alice Fryling, Editor

Notes

[1]Robert E. Webber, _The Majestic Tapestry_ (Nashville, Tenn.: Thomas Nelson Publishers, 1986), p. 134.

SECTION 1
UNDERSTANDING
DISCIPLEMAKING

1
WHAT IS DISCIPLEMAKING?

Ken died last summer. But Jim, the friend he nurtured, lives on. Jim is a Christian today and actively pursuing his place in the kingdom of God because Ken cared enough to help him become a disciple of Christ.

Jim met Ken before either of them was a Christian. In fact, at the time, Jim was only in the seventh grade. Ken was a teacher in his school and the minister of music in his church. That year a friendship began between teacher and student which lasted into Jim's adulthood. Their story is evidence of how God uses ordinary people for extraordinary purposes.

As their friendship grew, Ken began to help Jim develop his musical abilities. He convinced Jim that he could be a soloist. He influenced Jim's musical skills and taught him how to appreciate the world of art. He took him to concerts. He shared his record collection. They discussed politics, philosophy, history and art, even religion and the Bible.

And they had fun together. During long telephone conversations, they delighted in word games of their own creation. The Ant Dictionary was born during one of these conversations. In the Ant Dictionary, you will find such words as: *tyrant*—an exhausted ant. Or *russiant*—an ant in a hurry. Their goal was to "save the ants of America."

The Bubble Column, also born over the telephone wires, was later published in *HIS* magazine. In the Bubble Column were such words as *terribubble,* defined as "what the earth looks like from outer space," and *abominabubble,* "an explosive device hidden in a bubble."

During these early years of their friendship, Ken and Jim were not Christians. Ken acted like a Christian, but he struggled in the privacy of his mind and heart. As he looked at his life, he came to the point where he felt that he had two choices. One was to commit suicide. The other was to commit his life to Christ. He chose to become a Christian.

It was only natural, then, for Ken to tell Jim about what Jesus was doing in his life. Over the next few months Jim became convinced that he too needed to become a Christian. With Ken's guidance, Jim committed his life to Christ.

The nature of the friendship between Ken and Jim did not really change after that, but Ken began to focus part of their time and conversation on spiritual things. Ken wanted to see Jim grow as a Christian. They continued to share life, play together and learn together. They even took a trip to Europe one summer. They studied the Bible together. They prayed. Ken passed significant books on to Jim. Within the context of their friendship, Ken, a young Christian himself, discipled Jim, an even younger Christian.

The time came for Jim to graduate from high school and go off to college. Though Ken would not have that day-to-day contact with Jim anymore, he was still involved in his nurture. He prayed for him and wrote to him regularly. He sent him off to college with these final words of advice: "Get involved with a Christian group on campus. If you are going to survive as a Christian in college, you've got to be with others who are Christians too. They will help you continue to grow."

Ken had a vision for who Jim could become. As he launched Jim into adulthood, Ken gave him moorings to secure him in the faith. Ken's care, his prayers, his advice and his friendship all helped make Jim what he is today.

Ken died last year, a victim of a terminal illness, but Jim lives on, blossoming in Christ. Jim is committed to the pursuit of godliness, and he continues to influence men and women toward faith and growth in Jesus Christ. "The things you have heard me say in the presence of many witnesses entrust to reliable men who will also be qualified to teach others" (2 Tim 2:2). This is what Ken did for Jim. This is God's way of working out his plan for the world in the lives of individuals.

Influencing Others

Ken and Jim's story is unique only because Ken's early death adds poignancy to his ministry in Jim's life. Virtually all those people who are part of the kingdom today are there because their lives were touched by someone who cared. The influence of one person on another is not always as defined as Ken's influence on Jim. But do you know anyone who is a mature believer today whose life has not been touched by someone else's life? My own life has been touched by dozens of individuals whose examples and teaching prodded me on toward maturity.

There was my sister, who first told me that God loved me. There was the single woman who paid for me to go to a Christian conference when I was still in high school. There was the sophomore at college who invited me, a freshman, to a fellowship meeting. There was the friend who helped me in my first job and taught me about God's forgiveness. There was the pastor I'd never met who wrote an article that changed my way of thinking. There have been and continue to be many who influence me for Christ.

This influence is, in the broadest sense of the word, disciplemaking. Disciplemaking comes in many shapes and forms. College fellowship groups practice disciplemaking with Bible studies, conferences and large-group meetings. Churches practice disciplemaking with good teaching, fellowship opportunities and the observance of the sacraments. Writers disciple people with their books. Singers, with their music. Teachers, with their teaching.

But behind each public form of disciplemaking are individual people. And that's what this book is about. Friends discipling friends. People reaching out to neighbors, to family, perhaps even to strangers to proclaim Christ. With the apostle Paul, the modern-day disciplemaker says, "We want to be able to present each one to God, perfect because of what Christ has done for each of them" (Col 1:28b, Living Bible).

Disciplemaking, then, is the process of helping someone establish a relationship with Jesus and instructing that friend in the life of faith. In this book, we will focus primarily on the one-to-one form of disciplemaking. More specifically, we will focus on disciplemaking that is intentional, individualized and inspired.

Disciplemaking Is Intentional

Disciplemaking is intentional in that when we make disciples, we are following the example of Jesus in reaching out to people, taking initiative toward individuals who might become his disciples. Not all disciplemakers set out with the conscious intent of influencing potential disciples. But to be most effective, disciplemaking involves more than rubbing shoulders with friends—it is intentionally and actively helping them live on the growing edge of their faith.

Disciplemaking Is Individualized
Disciplemaking is individualized because no two people learn, change or grow in exactly the same way. Jesus sees us as unique individuals. He invites us, not to a philosophy or a program, but to a unique relationship with himself.

Effective disciplemaking is suited to that uniqueness. It does not come with a prefabricated formula. The process of disciplemaking is inductive; it develops and grows as we learn our friends' needs and interests.

Disciplemaking Is Inspired
And finally, disciplemaking is inspired. We cannot be effective disciplemakers if the Spirit of God is not at work in our lives and in the lives of those we disciple. We dare not approach discipling relationships without the confidence that the Holy Spirit lives in us so that our examples will be his example.

Disciplemaking is difficult. And it is rewarding. But the reward is that of the soldier fighting a battle, the athlete running the race or the farmer working hard to harvest a crop (2 Tim 2:3-6). If we are not inspired to be disciplemakers, we will not be able to do the job.

But when it is the Holy Spirit who inspires us, we can not only do the job, but do it with a zest and satisfaction that surpass any human effort. Disciplemakers use gifts God has given them. Paul Little, a man gifted by God with abilities in evangelism, wrote that he had met many Christian college students who lamented that their faith did not mean a thing to them. "My faith is like Pepsi that's lost its fizz."[1] When we are using the unique gifts God has given us, whatever the gifts are, we do indeed fizz like a newly opened bottle of Pepsi. Not everyone is gifted in relational ways. Not everyone has the ability to do one-on-one disciplemaking. But we all do have gifts that will help people grow as disciples, and when we use those gifts, the rewards are deep and satisfying.

The apostle Paul wrote that he worked with energy which God gave to him (Col 1:29). David wrote that responding to the Word of God had the effect of "reviving the soul" and "giving joy to the heart" (Ps 19:7-8). Jesus promised abundant life (Jn 10:10). What a privilege to receive from God energy and joy to do the work he asks us to do. For all of us, this work includes making disciples. For many of us, this will be through one-on-one relationships. We can expect that as we respond to God in obedience, he will indeed give us a "great reward" (Ps 19:11).

Notes
[1]Paul Little, *How to Give Away Your Faith*, rev. ed. (Downers Grove, Ill.: InterVarsity Press, 1988), p. 28.

Putting It All Together
1. Before you read this chapter, what were your ideas about discipleship?
How is the author's perspective different or the same as your own?
2. Think back over your life and recall two people who have most influenced you.
As you reflect on your relationship with those people, answer the following questions:
Why were you attracted to them?
How did they become significant in your life?
What do you appreciate most about them?
3. Examine the relationship between Jim and Ken. List the ways Ken influenced Jim.
Compare this list with the way your two friends influenced you.
What similarities and differences do you find?
What conclusions can you draw?
4. In this chapter the author describes taking initiative and being intentional in reaching out to a specific person to help that

person grow in Jesus. Are you a person who is willing to take initiative? Why or why not?

What prevents you from taking initiative sometimes?

5. Can you imagine yourself being an influencing person in someone else's life? Why or why not?

6. What do you want to learn about disciplemaking?

7. Pick either a soldier, athlete or farmer. In what ways do you think disciplemaking is similar or unlike that occupation?

8. Divide Colossians 1:28-29 into three sections. Rewrite each section in your own words.

2
DISCIPLEMAKING IS INTENTIONAL

I ran away when someone tried to disciple me. I was a freshman at college and had only been on campus a few weeks. The InterVarsity staff member visited campus to look me up. She asked if she could meet me at my dorm for dinner that night. I did not want to tell her that I was afraid to have her come. I was the new kid on the block. Our dorm was small and I was not sure strangers would be welcome. But rather than admit my fear, I agreed to have her come.

I went promptly back to my dorm, made arrangements for my roommate to greet my visitor, and then I left—to eat dinner out alone. I never told my staff member where I went. I simply ran away.

God's first disciple ran away too. God had just finished a beautiful garden that was to be home for Adam. He gave Adam food, flowers, trees, animals—even a companion and lover. But

Adam ran away, into the bushes. Adam knew he had disappoint-
ed God, but rather than admit his error, he tried to leave the
relationship.

Pursuit with Intent
The natural tendency of all men and women is to run away from
God. This makes disciplemaking a difficult task. I ran away.
Adam ran away. Peter ran from Jesus. John Mark ran from Paul.

Disciplemakers are almost always "it" in this game of hide-and-
seek. As disciplemakers, we will frequently find ourselves looking
for people who are hiding from God. Often, they are just waiting
to be found. They remind me of a story my friend Margaret told
me.

Margaret had had a disagreement with Phil. In jest, he had
locked her out of his office on campus where they were both
studying. She put a note under the door. He responded with
another note, slipped under the still-locked door. Suddenly, without either one realizing what was happening, the joke became an
argument. Margaret was hurt. Phil didn't catch it. So Margaret
went down the hall to a large lecture room and set up camp just
inside the door.

What she didn't know was that she was inside the door just
enough for Phil not to see her when he came looking. He
searched the whole building. Then he panicked. He went to
Margaret's apartment. Her roommate hadn't seen her. He called
one of her good friends. She didn't know where Margaret was,
either. They both joined Phil in the search, picking up a few more
friends en route. Finally, they went back to the classroom building
where it all started. They found Margaret in tears in Phil's office,
waiting to be found.

Our friends may be like that. At first, Margaret didn't even
realize she was running away. By the time she did, it was almost
too late to be found. But Phil loved Margaret. He was determined

to find her, and deep inside, she wanted to be found. But as she sat in the lecture hall, all she felt was fear at what she had done and anxiety about what would happen. Phil's determination to find her reassured Margaret that their relationship was secure.

One of the things that Scripture makes very clear is that God too is determined to find us. When he finds us, he seldom chides us for running away. He never accuses us for being afraid. He accepts us where we are. And he replaces our fear with a vision of what we can be.

Vision for a New Creation

We see this intentional initiative in the ministry of Jesus. Jesus' ministry was not a game. Nor was it as simple as a lovers' quarrel. But we can see in his life the intentionality of someone looking out for others. He actively sought out those he chose to love. He didn't sit in a carpenter shop with a welcome sign on the door. He looked for his disciples in trees and fishing boats and other ordinary places. Then he intentionally helped them become new people, the people he envisioned them to be.

Look at the way he reached out to Zaccheus, a turncoat Jew who got rich working for the hated Roman government by cheating his own people. We probably would not have liked Zaccheus very well. He was short, so short that when he heard that Jesus would be passing by, he had to climb up into a tree to be able to see him. He probably hoped to be a silent, unnoticed observer. He knew how the crowd would treat him if they noticed him there. But Jesus had other ideas. He invited himself to Zaccheus's home for lunch. He saw Zaccheus not as a hated tax collector but as a host with the potential to be a disciple. The results? Salvation came where the Jews might have least expected it.

And look at the way Jesus captivated Peter, helping him see who he could become. Peter was no saint. At least he was no saint in the way we normally think of one. And if anyone was aware of Peter's shortcomings, it was Jesus. Who was too busy cleaning his nets to pay close attention to Jesus' teaching? Peter. Who had the nerve to tell the Messiah not to go around telling people he might get killed by the Pharisees because it wasn't the politically shrewd thing to do? Peter. Who protested one minute that he would never let Jesus wash his feet and the next minute insisted that Jesus give him a complete bath? Peter, again. Who used his sword to defend the Prince of Peace when a group of soldiers came to arrest Jesus? And who, hours later, denied to an unarmed maiden that he ever knew Jesus? Of course, it was Peter.

This picture of impetuous, hot-one-minute-cold-the-next Peter makes the name Jesus picked for him all that much more ironic. Would you call your most unpredictable friend "Peter"—the Greek word for *rock*? Jesus did. It's like calling Susan, who is always late for everything, "Speedy." Or calling Hal, who always manages to see the worst possibilities in life, "Happy." But Jesus was doing more than teasing his good friend. When he called Peter "The Rock," he was envisioning the best that Peter could be and trying to build that same vision into Peter himself.

His vision of Peter was so hopeful that Jesus said to him: "Blessed are you, Simon son of Jonah. . . . I tell you that you are Peter, and on this rock I will build my church, and the gates of Hades will not overcome it. I will give you the keys of the kingdom of heaven; whatever you bind on earth will be bound in heaven, and whatever you loose on earth will be loosed in heaven" (Mt 16:17-19).

I don't know about you, but if I had been calling the shots, the keys to the kingdom would not have gone to this unreliable fisherman.

Of course we all know how Peter turned out. He still had his problems, but he did indeed become one of the pillars of the early church. Eventually he died for his faith, remaining true to his master, faithful to the end. And it all started because Jesus saw potential in a hotheaded Galilean and began to build that vision into him. When I disciple people, I know that I can't look just at their faults and weaknesses. Nor can I give into their fears. I must ask Jesus to show me who it is they will become in Christ, and then I need to keep this clearly in my mind.

Consider one more story which shows Jesus' ability to seek out people, to see potential and to bring it out in them. The Samaritan woman at the well was the kind of person most of us today would avoid at all costs (Jn 4:4-26). She had been divorced five times. On top of this, she was living with her current boyfriend. But Jesus reached out to her. He accepted her as she was. He simply loved her. He took her questions seriously. He talked with her, graciously and honestly. He did not shrink from pointing out her sin, but he didn't center his attention on all the reasons why she would be a poor candidate for the evangelism committee. Instead he had a vision for who she could be. And within a matter of minutes, she was indeed bringing a whole town to meet the Savior.

Vision for Growth

If we want to be disciplemakers, then, we must follow Jesus' example and intentionally seek out those who are waiting to grow. We need to communicate that Jesus loves each of us as we are and that he will help us become much more than we think we can ever be. We must not be put off if those we reach out to seem to be hiding. For their sakes and for the sake of the kingdom of God, we must take time to think of what they could be if they came out of hiding. Then we need to seek them out, to love them with Jesus' love and to intentionally help them grow to become disciples of the King.

Watching a disciple being born and seeing that new person grow is exciting. But sometimes it is frustrating. Growth is not perpetual motion. It is more like mountain climbing, with steep inclines, plateaus and vistas along the way. As disciplemakers, we need to be as intentional as mountain climbers are about reaching the summit. We need to help young Christians keep going when they tire out. We need to prod them on when they stop too long at plateaus. And we need to help them enjoy the scenery as they go.

Let me give a twentieth-century example of a new disciple learning to climb the mountain. Don Murphy became a Christian soon after he visited a Bible study I had in the men's dorm on a campus near where I lived.

Don and I talked at length, and I rejoiced when he became a new creature in Christ. But I knew that his newfound relationship with Jesus was just a beginning. We were at the foothills of the mountain. Don is married, and I was quite sure his wife would be less than enthusiastic about his new faith. He also had a little more than his fair share of emotional baggage, which he had been carrying around since childhood. He lives in a materialistic world, and I did not think it would be easy for him to let go of the security he sought in money. Spiritual disciplines were almost foreign to him. In deciding to follow Jesus, Don was embracing a whole new way of thinking. The mountain ahead was steep.

As I thought about how I could help him in the climb, I thought of at least six areas where he would need support. I did not zap him with a six-point program, nor did I think I would be the only one God would use in his life. But in my own mind, I hoped to see Don grow (1) in knowing God's love and forgiveness more fully; (2) in his prayer life; (3) in his understanding of Scripture; (4) in his everyday experience of the lordship of Jesus; (5) in sharing his faith with others; and (6) in developing a biblical value system.

Admittedly, these six areas are easier to see with hindsight. At the time, the main thing I did to facilitate growth, to climb the mountain with Don, was to give him time—lots of time. The areas of growth were woven together as we prayed together and had Bible studies together and as I listened for hours while Don worked through past emotional problems. I supported him as he tried to meet the daily crises of his life.

But Don supported me too. As I gave time to Don, he in turn stood by me in my own crises. One of the joys of disciplemaking is that those God calls us to disciple almost always become our friends, reflecting back to us the love of God. I found that I could call Don and ask him to pray about a specific need in my life. Many times our Bible studies taught me new truths for my own life. And Don was willing to reach out to help me and listen to me when I needed to talk. In fact, it has been very important for Don to know that our friendship has this mutual dimension.

Looking back (with the benefit of a mountaineer's hindsight), I can see how Don has grown in experiencing God's love. Even after he became a Christian, Don often had a hard time believing God really loved him and found pleasure in him. But he is growing in this area. And with the more secure moorings of God's love in his life, Don is beginning to work through relationships that have been difficult. Various broken family relationships and friendships are being restored as he has taken initiative to bring about healing. Up to the time of his conversion, he had just ignored these relationships. Now he is reaching out in forgiveness and reconciliation.

Don is also discovering that the Word of God has the power to change his life. One of the first things we did together was to meet every day for a quiet time, reading the Bible and praying together. Then we met together just once a week. Even now Don will occasionally ask me to share his quiet time. He is also studying the Bible with others and is under the teaching of the Word in his church.

Don increasingly prays for others and for his world. Gradually, his prayers are more full of worship, gratitude and thanksgiving.

And as he prays, his faith is growing.

As Don is growing, he is learning what it means to live under God's authority. He sees that obedience to Jesus Christ is not optional. But, as Don is finding out, this is not always easy. He is learning, for example, that being a servant to others is hard, especially when our service is not appreciated. But Jesus calls us to servanthood, and Don knows there is no option. He is working on this in several relationships.

Because God's Word teaches that we are to meet with other Christians for worship, fellowship and teaching, Don recognized that he must make a commitment to his local church. I have seen his appreciation for the church grow. Worship and communion have taken on new significance. The first time he took communion after his conversion, he said, "I didn't know it could be so meaningful! I feel like I have taken communion for the very first time. I guess it is the first time!" Now he is beginning to ask how his gifts can be used in his church.

I envision Don being part of that process Paul described where one Christian shares with others who will in turn teach more (2 Tim 2:2). It was exciting to see Don begin to wonder, "How can I live so Richard will be drawn to Jesus?" and "How can I live my life so Brian will want to be even more obedient to Christ because of being with me?" He is finding out that witnessing and discipling are not means of controlling another person but rather of influencing another's walk with God. He sees that we are called to make disciples, not just new Christians.

Finally, my vision for Don has included his becoming a person who does not isolate his spirituality from the rest of life. He is developing kingdom values. He is becoming more aware of evil in the world, whether it is in the form of materialism, racism, war or immorality. He is learning how to stand against it. Don is beginning to know how to integrate a Christian perspective on the job and to establish habits that will lead to good physical and emotional, as well as spiritual, health.

The areas of growth I envisioned for Don are similar to those I picture for other young believers—and for myself. The transformation in lives today is no less than it was in the days of Peter and Zaccheus. But for each of us, there will be different points of emphasis. And at different seasons of life, we will be growing in different areas. I try to see where God is at work in my life, and where he is at work in the lives of my friends, and then I pray for and encourage growth in those particular areas.

Sometimes I feel overwhelmed when I think of trying to influence someone in this way. I wonder just who I think I am. Or I fear that I will not be up to the task. Sometimes the Dons in my life back off, and then I get discouraged. But God himself is at work. And he is using many people to accomplish his purposes. I am just one person in Don's life. I have had to learn to live with the tension of taking my influence on Don's life seriously enough to be intentional, but not so seriously that I think that Don's growth depends totally on me.

Parents of young children often feel that they are sculpting the future generation. Sometimes disciplemakers take themselves this seriously too. But child psychologists tell us that the influence of parents is *not* like sculpting. Parents do radically influence a child's development, but the parent does not shape and form the final product as a sculptor creates his art. Rather, psychologists tell us, it is as though the parent falls on the damp clay and leaves an indelible impression.

I need to remember that as I seek to disciple people. God is the potter. He is creating me too. I make an impression, and Jesus wants me to do that. But he takes my work, my impression, and combines it with the impressions of others to mold each of us into his own work of art.

I never thought I could be an artist, but God has allowed me to stand beside his potter's wheel—a wonderful place to be.

Putting It All Together

1. Describe a time when someone took initiative to do something for you before you had to ask. How did you feel about what your friend did?

2. Just for fun, describe the last time you remember playing hide-and-seek. How old were you? What was your favorite hiding place?

3. When have you ever hidden from God? Describe how you felt while you were in hiding.

4. What is one area of your life where you discovered you had more potential than you thought you did? Who helped you make that discovery? What helped you grow in that area?

5. Think of a friend who is a young Christian. Ask Jesus to show you what potential he sees in your friend. What can you do to help your friend grow in being a disciple and in developing that potential?

6. Pick one of the disciples described in this chapter, Simon Peter (Lk 5:1-11), Zacchaeus (Lk 19:1-16) or the Samaritan woman (Jn 4:7-36). Take a minute or two and imagine yourself living life as that person lived it. What do you think you would have been thinking when Jesus approached you? How do you think you might have responded to him? Why do you think each of these people said yes to Jesus?

3
DISCIPLEMAKING IS INDIVIDUALIZED

W_hat do a tax collector, a fisher-_
man, a live-in mistress and a college student have in common?
In the case of Zaccheus, Peter, the Samaritan woman and my
friend Don, they have almost nothing in common—except that
they have all met Jesus.

We are apprenticed to a perfect artist. No two pieces of work
are exactly alike. Disciples do not come from factories, and neither do disciplemakers. We cannot treat people like projects,
shaping new disciples according to our own abilities and intentions, according to a preconceived plan. Rather, we bring ourselves and our friends to Jesus, the eternal potter, who shapes us
into unique, useful and beautiful vessels.

Disciplemaking is individualized. Every disciple grows differently, and every disciplemaker nurtures with a little different
emphasis. I don't know exactly what a discipling relationship will

look like for you or your disciple, because individuals are all different. But it is the same God who works in all of us.

Let me tell you how this individual process is happening in the life of my friend Jeanette.

Jeanette came to town yesterday. She is so special that it was not hard for me to jump out of bed for our 5:00 A.M. date. As we sat sipping coffee at the best breakfast spot in town, I was amazed and grateful at what I saw. Here before me sat a mature woman of Christ. We had a lot in common when we first met twelve years ago. We were both Christians. We were both in the nursing profession. We both loved music. We were serious about life and relationships, and we each had a passion for Baskin Robbins pralines-and-cream ice-cream cones.

At that time Jeanette was a young Christian, with many difficulties in her life. One problem was her relationship with her mother. It was full of bitterness and conflict, as it had been for many years. Jeanette found it easier to blame her mother for the strain in their communication than to look closely and see the problem as having two sides to it.

She also had difficulty sharing her faith. It frightened her to think about the possibility of being rejected by her family and friends. They might see her as a religious fanatic. And she was afraid of being asked questions that she might not be able to answer. She did not want to risk intruding into someone's life where she was not wanted.

Spending time alone with God was hard. Because she had a difficult time believing that God loved her, she did not know that God enjoyed her company, that he wanted to be with her. She knew that Jesus died for her sins and that he loved the world. But she could not believe that he valued her and that her attention and praise brought him pleasure. Time alone with God was not a joyful experience of being with a loved one but an opportunity for God to tell her all that was wrong with her.

As a matter of fact, Jeanette had trouble believing that anyone loved her. She did not like herself. And because she did not like herself, she assumed that other people did not like her. She kept people at a safe distance emotionally. She was not going to give them a chance to hurt her by showing that they did not like her. Part of her self-protection involved acting as if she did not care what others felt or thought. She doubted that anyone truly enjoyed her. As a result, sometimes she trusted me, and at other times it was a challenge to effectively communicate my care for her.

Now, twelve years later, we were sitting together for breakfast as the sun rose. What changes had taken place in her since that time when we first met! As we talked, it became obvious that her fear of evangelism was gone. Many people had heard about Jesus through her. The fabric of her conversation revealed the depth of her daily contact with God. Here before me was a person who was comfortable to be with because she was now so comfortable with herself. She had come to accept God's unconditional acceptance of her.

God's Personalized Work

What had brought about this remarkable change? Had she found the glass slipper and been transformed overnight like Cinderella? Not at all. She was the product of God's patient work in her life steadily over the years. Our friendship was one part of that work. God brought Jeanette into my life at a time when she needed nurturing in her relatively new Christian faith. Concern for her spiritual growth flowed very naturally out of the special love for her that God had given to me.

Now God was allowing me to see evidence of fruit resulting from a relationship in which a primary goal was to help Jeanette to mature in Jesus Christ, as well as to be her good friend. Even more than this, he was allowing me to see his great faithfulness.

His work in Jeanette began before I ever arrived on the scene, and it continued after I left. Over the years the Holy Spirit was producing God's character in her.

From the beginning, Jeanette and I enjoyed sharing life and getting to know each other better. As we shared ourselves, we shared our relationship with the Lord Jesus. We had fun. Some of our activities were done with the specific goal that Jesus' character be developed in Jeanette. The issue became not just to learn to *do* things but to *be* who God wanted us to be. The question was not what *skills* we should develop, but *who* we should become. And as Jeanette grew and was changed by God, I also grew and was changed by God.

Even though I was the "mentor" in the relationship, I was growing and changing in many of the same ways as Jeanette. My experience of quiet time deepened as I helped her establish a quiet time. My understanding of human nature grew as I watched Jeanette learn to love her parents more. My appreciation for God's sovereignty in evangelism grew as I saw how he worked through Jeanette. But I am getting ahead of myself. . . .

At first, Jeanette and I began by working on a daily quiet time. We met for prayer and Bible study each morning at 6:00 A.M., taking turns fixing the coffee. I had already given her the Inter-Varsity Press booklet *Quiet Time*. We discussed it and prayed together that first morning. We used a hymnal to sing songs of worship to God. After several days of showing her what a quiet time was like and discussing why it's important to meet with God on a regular basis, we stopped meeting daily, and only got together occasionally for a quiet time after that.

When we weren't meeting for regular quiet times, we would discuss what we were learning in our times alone with God. We would share difficulties we were having in applying God's Word to our daily lives. We shared prayer requests and answers to prayer.

Jeanette told me how hard it was for her to believe God loved her personally. She sobbed as she shared about her sexual involvement with a young man she had dated in high school. This had happened before she had become a Christian. She had confessed it to God many times. Though she knew the facts about God's forgiveness, she had not accepted that she was forgiven. She felt pain and failure. She still felt unloved by God.

We looked at what the Bible had to say in Romans 8 and discussed the truth that nothing separated her from God's love. We talked about the fact that God gave Jesus to Jeanette to die for her sins. Therefore he would also give her all things with him (v. 32). That included a clean slate, an open and loving relationship with himself, and a freed conscience. Psalm 139 communicated clearly God's personal attention to her. We looked at passages about God calling Jeanette by name and claiming her as his own. Through the Gospels we saw the cross with fresh perspective. We sang together the words from a hymn: "In tenderness He sought me, weary and sick with sin. And on his shoulders brought me back to his fold again. . . . Oh the love that sought me, oh the blood that bought me, oh the grace that brought me to the fold" (W. S. Walton, 1894).

Jeanette told me later that was a turning point in her Christian life. These experiences are hard to put into words, but she said that for the first time she was able to accept and receive God's personal love for her. She experienced freedom from guilt and freedom to celebrate her relationship with God. As she became secure in God's love, she began to love and accept herself. Then she could allow herself to be loved and accepted by others around her.

One Person to the Next
Telling others about our faith in Christ was another topic that Jeanette and I discussed from time to time. We attended seminars

on "Meeting Spiritual Needs," "Death" and "Friendship Evangelism." We prayed for our non-Christian friends. She saw me in-
teract with non-Christian friends and acquaintances.

On one occasion we attended a professional convention together. In the morning before we left, Jeanette read what Paul
wrote in Colossians 4:3, "And pray for us, too, that God may open
a door for our message, so that we may proclaim the mystery of
Christ." She decided to ask God to do that for her.

Karen, the president of the convention, traveled with us and
shared our motel room. As the lights went out in our room that
first night, Karen began asking questions about spiritual things.
We ended up talking about John 14 and Jesus' claim to be the
way, truth and life. Karen did not become a Christian that evening, but it certainly had an impact on Jeanette. In that conversation Jeanette saw a natural way of communicating faith in
Christ to an unbeliever.

Sometime later Jeanette had another door opened for her to
declare the mystery of Christ to a patient in her care. She ended
up using the same passage of Scripture that we used in that room
with Karen. Jeanette's patient made a commitment to Christ as
a result of their conversation.

Jeanette and I did not see each other as often after that. But
God continued to work in her life. The morning we met for coffee
in my hometown, she told me the remarkable story of what was
happening between her and her parents. After many years, her
relationship with her mother had not substantially improved.
And to make matters worse, the warm relationship she had had
with her father, Bill, had deteriorated because of the ongoing
tension between her and her mother.

But now her mother was battling a terminal illness in the hospital. Jeanette had come home to visit. She was irritated with her
father. She thought the breakdown in their relationship was his
fault. But God began to speak to her about her own responsibility

to break the negative patterns of communication that had developed. It was not all his problem.

She prayed, and as she prayed, she decided to talk to her father. Gently she shared her feelings with him. His response: "What use is there, anyway? Things around here have gone from bad to worse."

"What do you mean?" she asked.

Slowly he began to reveal deep feelings. He talked about how hard it had been on him to have so much tension between Jeanette and her mother, about the anguish of his wife's illness, about the stress of driving two hours to the hospital to visit and support her, about the demands of keeping up with harvesting a large farm in the midst of everything else.

On top of that, he had told off one of his best friends, Henry, over some issue which now seemed unimportant. He grieved the loss of the friendship. He had regretted his harsh words and hasty action.

Finally he said, "And I have asked God for forgiveness in all of these situations, and what good does it do? Nothing changes."

Jeanette sensed his deep pain and realized he had been suffering a long time. She wept. He had never talked to her like this before. Finally she said, "Dad, have you ever committed your life to Jesus Christ?"

He told her that he hadn't, but he said he didn't want his stubbornness to keep him from Jesus any longer. The next morning they visited a local pastor whom Jeanette's father could respect and who knew the Lord intimately. The pastor shared clearly about God's love for Bill and what it meant to become a Christian. As her father prayed and asked Jesus into his heart, he sobbed. The pastor put his arms around this big Kansas farmer and said, "Sir, these are good tears."

That evening on the phone he told his wife he had committed his life to the Lord. "And," he continued, "I hope Jeanette can help you in the same way."

As she talked with Jeanette after that call, her mother made a clear statement of faith in Jesus Christ and talked about when she had become a Christian. She also was able to express to Jeanette how important Jeanette was to her and that she did want and need to have her around.

When Jeanette recounted this story to me, gratitude flooded over me like the waves that come over me when I am playing in the ocean. Once again, good tears flowed. Jeanette and I wept together, tears of joy over what God had done.

Jeanette's story is the story of someone who learned to follow Jesus. It is typical of the way God works to use one disciple to influence another disciple. According to Eugene Peterson, "A disciple is a learner, but not in the academic setting of the school room, rather at the worksite of a craftsman. We do not acquire information about God but rather skills in faith."[1]

Jeanette and I were, first of all, friends. As our friendship grew, she was able to see God's good work in my life. I was able to share with her my own efforts to respond to his work. We read Scripture and prayed together. We focused on how God could heal some of the hurts in her life. And we shared experiences of communicating our faith to others. (We also continued to eat ice-cream cones together!)

Jeanette was not a project or a burden to me. God planted in my heart a longing to see her grow. And he gave me a longing to serve her. Because this relationship was God's idea, the friendship enriched my life as well as Jeanette's. It was exciting to see Jeanette grow. And I grew along with her.

My times with Jeanette are not frequent now. She lives across the country from me. But she is still a very special friend. I like seeing God use her as an agent of change in her own family. There is evidence of her having a vital role in the lives of students on the university campus where she is now teaching. She is influencing faculty and staff in spiritual things, helping them to consider their own spiritual needs as well as those of their students. In Jeanette's life, before my eyes, I am seeing the truth of 2 Timothy 2:2 being lived out: "And the things you have heard me say in the presence of many witnesses entrust to reliable men who will also be qualified to teach others." This is discipling.

Notes
[1]Eugene Peterson, *A Long Obedience in the Same Direction* (Downers Grove, Ill.: InterVarsity Press, 1980), p. 13.

Putting It All Together
1. The author observed five aspects of her relationship with Jeanette which God used to help Jeanette grow.

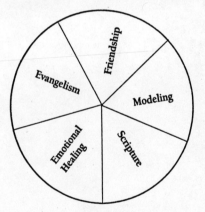

2. What about your own gifts? In what areas do you feel you have the most to offer a young Christian?
What things do you do which help other people grow in these areas?
3. Which aspect of disciplemaking looks the most difficult to you?
What is one thing you could do in each area you listed in ques-

tion 2 to sharpen your ability to be helpful to a new believer?

4. Think of the relationships in your own life which have helped you mature in your faith. Describe one way you have experienced the truths of the following verses in a relationship with someone else.

1 Thess 2:8
1 Cor 11:1
Jn 15:10-11
2 Cor 1:3-4
2 Tim 2:2

5. Think of a young Christian friend whom you might disciple. Write down that person's name.

In each of the five areas from question 2, write down one way you could reach out to your friend.

4
DISCIPLEMAKING IS INSPIRED

I am fascinated with how God works in people's lives. I love to stand at his potter's wheel and watch. Only God can know how each person needs to be shaped and molded, with what tool and at what speed.

Despite my joy at his work, there are times when I get discouraged. There are times when I say, "This is too much. I can't disciple all these people. They're a bunch of sinners anyway. It takes too long. It's too hard. I'm sorry, but I give up."

Then, once again, I run and hide. At times like this, I hide behind discouragement and depression. God has found me there over and over again. When he finds me, he reminds me that disciplemaking is not my idea. It is his. He is the potter. It is not my ability that matters. It is his. It is not my timetable, but his, that he is using. And the result is not personal achievement but the joy of working alongside the Creator God.

His Idea

One of the reminders that disciplemaking is God's idea and not mine is a starry sky on a clear night. I remember how exciting it was as a child to be able to identify the stars in Orion's belt. My life's work in astronomy was launched. I had come a long way from the days of "Twinkle, Twinkle, Little Star." Unfortunately, my career in astronomy ended as quickly as it began. As far as names go, I still only know Orion and his belt. But I see something else in the stars now that I did not see as a child. I see God's promise.

God promised Abraham, one of the first disciples, that he would bless Abraham. He said to him: "I will . . . make your descendants as numerous as the stars in the sky and as the sand on the seashore. . . . Through your offspring all nations on earth will be blessed, because you have obeyed me" (Gen 22:17-18). This was not an extravagant promise, made to be forgotten. It was true. And in this promise is the seed of my own conviction that disciplemaking is not my idea, but God's.

About 4,000 years ago, God told Abraham about his plan. Abraham lived in Haran. God told him to move to Canaan. God said, "I will make you into a great nation and I will bless you; I will make your name great, and you will be a blessing. . . . All peoples on earth will be blessed through you" (Gen 12:2-3). God's intention, starting with Abraham, has been to bless all peoples of the earth. When I look at the stars, I remember his promise. When I disciple someone, I am participating in that plan.

Let's take a brief look at the unfolding of God's intentions in history. Notice how many times he repeats his promise to draw all people to himself and to bless them as they come to know him.

Almost 600 years after Abraham lived, Joshua led the Israelites across the Jordan River. On the other side of the river, he built a memorial to remind the people that "the LORD your God dried up the Jordan before [us] until [we] had crossed over. He did this so that all the peoples of the earth might know that the hand of the LORD is powerful and so that you might always fear the LORD your God" (Josh 4:23-24). His plan with Abraham and with Joshua was that all people would know him as Lord.

Another few hundred years later we see Solomon, following in the footsteps of his father, King David. Receiving instructions from God to build a temple, Solomon directed a team of people to completion of the task. Then he dedicated the temple with a reminder. The temple, he said, was to be a house of prayer and worship. It was also to be used for sacrifices for the atonement of sin. Solomon concludes, "May the LORD our God be with us as he was with our fathers; may he never leave us nor forsake us . . . that all the peoples of the earth may know that the LORD is God." (1 Kings 8:57, 60).

The implication is that there was an even greater purpose for the temple than prayers and sacrifices. The temple was to proclaim the Almighty God to the world. The temple was to tell the world that there is a living, loving God who cares for them and desires a relationship with them.

Centuries later, Jesus said this about himself: "I tell you that one greater than the temple is here" (Mt 12:6). And this: "I, when I am lifted up from the earth, will draw all men to myself" (Jn 12:32). Jesus has been doing that ever since.

His apostle Paul wrote to the first-century church: "And he made known to us the mystery of his will according to his good pleasure, which he purposed in Christ, to be put into effect when the times will have reached their fulfillment—to bring all things in heaven and on earth together under one head, even Christ" (Eph 1:9-10).

Finally, in Revelation 21, John saw a new heaven and a new earth. And he "heard a loud voice from the throne saying, 'Now the dwelling of God is with men, and he will live with them. They will be his people, and God himself will be with them and be their God' " (Rev 21:3).

From beginning to end, Scripture describes a remarkable plan: God intends to dwell in men and women and to draw all of us to himself. From Adam and Eve hiding in the bushes to John envisioning a new heaven and a new earth, God's intent has been to "bring . . . salvation to the ends of the earth" (Is 49:6). As we become disciplemakers, we are merely participating in what God has been doing for thousands of years.

His Ability
Seeing God at work throughout biblical history inspires me. It also helps me when I am discouraged. God got along without me before he met me, so he is not dependent on my ability, my winsomeness or my inspiration to fulfill his plan. But in his graciousness, he allows me to participate in what he is doing.

I identify with Gideon. Gideon was the soldier God used to lead the Israelites against their enemies, the Midianites. Gideon was not a picture of courage and inspiration. He was, rather, tentative and indecisive. When God called him to lead the army, Gideon was busy hiding from the enemy in a winepress. An angel of the Lord came to him and said, "The LORD is with you, mighty warrior" (Judg 6:12). Had I been Gideon, I think I would have looked over my shoulder to see if there was a mighty warrior behind my back! I don't know what God saw in Gideon that identified him as a future leader, but history validates God's choice.

There are times when I don't see what God sees in me to qualify me to be a disciplemaker. But every now and then someone comes along and talks to me the way the angel talked to Gideon.

This happened to me last Thursday. I was discouraged. I convinced myself that I didn't know how to disciple anyone. And I was tired of trying. In the mail that day I found a letter from a student. She wrote,

As I look back on my growth as a person over the last year and a half, I can say that much of that growth has been aided by you. You ask very good questions which make me think and you speak words of truth that continue to challenge me to change.

When I read the letter, I had an impulse to double-check the envelope to see if it had come to the right person.

God used that letter to restore my enthusiasm for being a disciplemaker. I was reminded again that my confidence cannot be in my own ability but in God's. He works in me, beyond what I can imagine, to do his will (see Phil 2:13 and Eph 3:20).

One of the reasons I know this is true is because I have experienced the "boomerang effect" of disciplemaking. It is a fascinating phenomenon. A boomerang flies out to its target and returns to its thrower. Similarly, there have been many times when I have helped younger Christians solve problems, learn truths from Scripture or understand God's love in a new way. Later, when I have had to solve problem, learn truths or experience God's love, my young Christian friends have helped me in the very same ways I helped them. Sometimes I have even gone so far as to say, "Now what did I say to you when you were working on this?" Perhaps this is part of the truth hidden in the verse, "Cast your bread upon the waters, for after many days you will find it again" (Eccles 11:1). God in his kindness speaks back to me the very truths he first spoke through me.

His Timetable

Disciplemaking, then, is God's idea and based on his ability. It also runs according to his timetable. Some fruit in disciplemaking comes as quickly as squash in a summer garden. Other fruit, like the oak tree in our front yard, takes years to develop. The rate of growth is God's, not ours.

The story of Abraham is especially helpful when I become

impatient. Ten years after God promised Abraham that he would be the father of a great nation, he and Sarah were still childless. Abraham and Sarah were confused. So confused that they decided to take things into their own hands. It seemed logical to help God out by Abraham having a child with Sarah's servant Hagar (Gen 15 and 16). But disaster and tragedy followed this "logical conclusion."

But God didn't give up on Abraham. Thirteen years after Hagar's son, Ishmael, was born, God repeated his promise to Abraham (Gen 17:1-2). Twenty-five years after his initial promise, God gave Abraham a son, Isaac (Gen 21:1-3). Isaac was to be in the genealogical line of Jesus, and today, as we seek to make disciples for Jesus, we are part of the fulfillment of God's promise to Abraham 4,000 years ago.

I think too of Timothy's mother, Eunice, and his grandmother, Lois (2 Tim 1:5). I don't know what Timothy was like as a little boy. But I know what little boys are like today, and I can imagine that there were times when Eunice and Lois despaired that their boy would ever grow up, let alone become a minister of the gospel. But God knew how he wanted to use Timothy. And God knew who Timothy would become. God was at work in Timothy's life years before anyone else knew.

Or consider John Mark, one of the early disciples. It must have been a discouraging time when he walked out on Paul (Acts 13:13; 15:37-49). Only God knew that John Mark would come back, stronger than ever—though his cousin Barnabas may have believed it, and that belief may have played a part in John Mark's eventual about-face.

Disciplemaking, then, is the continuation of God's work throughout history. We may not have the privilege of seeing all the fruit of our work. Sometimes we see enough to encourage us, as I did when I read the letter from the student. But some fruit takes thirteen, twenty-five, even seventy-five years to ripen. God is at work in individuals. He is at work in history. If we are receptive to his ways, he uses us to do his work.

Disciplemaking is not something nice to do if we have time. It is one of the most important things we can do in our lives. Disciplemaking is nothing less than aligning ourselves with God's creative intention of blessing all the people on earth (Gen 12:1-3). Disciplemaking is an inspired plan.

The Joy of Disciplemaking

Because disciplemaking is his idea, his work in his time, there is great satisfaction for the disciplemaker. It's true that when I give myself to disciple others, I give up a lot. I give up my time. Often, I give up my own agenda for their sakes. I invest myself in things that are important to them, rather than to me. I let go of values important to the world—the pay being low and the results sometimes slow. But in the end, I gain more than I ever lose.

Perhaps this is part of what Jesus meant when he said that we need to lose life in order to gain life (Mt 16:25). Working to build the kingdom is at the core of my purpose for being, and disciplemaking is at the core of that kingdom-building work. When I "make disciples," according to Jesus' instructions (Mt 28:19-20), I am living life as he intended for me to live it. Because he is a good God, a loving, generous Father, much of the compensation for my work is immediate. There is the pleasure of seeing others find comfort as they realize God loves them. There is the excitement of seeing them find peace as they step out in an act of practical obedience. There is the warmth of fellowship with those I disciple. Most of all, there is the sheer joy of knowing that God smiles as he looks at what I am doing.

God's Word, the long-term signs of fruit, the feedback of others and the peace of obedience have convinced me that disciplemaking is an inspired plan, a divine lifestyle.

Putting It All Together

1. How convinced are you that God is really at work in the world today?

Not at all convinced _____ Very convinced

Put an X on the spot where you see yourself.

2. King Solomon prayed that "all the peoples of the earth may know that the LORD is God" (1 Kings 8:60). When you are tempted to doubt that Jesus is Lord of the world, what specific things help to restore your faith?

3. Think of a person you know who acts as though he or she believes that God is active in history. What is distinctive about how that person responds to everyday life?

4. What are some specific ways you have seen God intersect your own life recently?

5. When are you most apt to get discouraged in your disciple-making efforts?

6. Write a modern-day paraphrase for each of the following verses:

 Ephesians 1:9-10
 Philippians 2:13
 Matthew 16:25

5

AUTHORITY AND TRUTH: BEYOND CULTURAL BARRIERS

When I suggested to small-group leaders at Arizona State University that we begin to train and encourage students to disciple other students in the larger group, I was met with an outcry of resistance. Each student had something negative to say. They felt awkward. They feared imposing unwanted ideas on others. They did not want to be in a relationship where one person seemed "above" another. No way, they told me, did they want to be involved in individual discipling relationships with their fellow students.

These students reflected the mood of our society, which is in sharp contrast with Jesus' final instructions. Jesus' parting words at the end of his ministry on earth were: "Go and make disciples. . . . [Teach] them to obey everything I have commanded you" (Mt 28:19-20). Jesus' plan for the growth of his church was that his disciples would teach other men and women how to be disciples and that those men and women would, in turn, teach others. Sometime between the first century A.D. and today, Jesus' words have been watered down to: "Sit tight and live your life so that others will see you are my disciples. Perhaps they too can figure out how to follow me."

What happened to the sense of commission that Jesus gave to his students? The book of Acts and the letters to the early churches describe some of the attempts of the first disciples to follow through on Jesus' intentions. What happened to their sense of calling? What happened to the idea of taking initiative to help someone become a disciple?

I believe that our commitment to be disciplemakers has faded in the glare of two pervasive attitudes in our society. It has faded in light of our attitudes toward authority and truth.

Attitudes toward Authority

The students at ASU told me that they did not want to be disciplemakers because they did not want to appear to be "above" anyone else. Abuse of authority in our society has caused sensitive people to shy away from assuming a position of personal authority in another's life. The process of disciplemaking is not in itself an authoritative process. The disciplemaker does not tell the new disciple what to do. But the disciplemaker does represent Jesus, who claimed "all authority in heaven and on earth" (Mt 28:18). Whether my student friends at ASU were conscious of it or not, they responded intuitively to the recognition that disciplemaking means helping their friends come to grips with the authority of Jesus in their lives.

One of the tragedies of the twentieth century is that most people have not experienced authority in a positive sense. In the family we have seen marital and parental abuse; in the church, pastoral abuse; and in government, political abuse. It is no wonder, then, that bumper stickers and T-shirts, whether explicitly or implicitly, tell us to "Question Authority."

In the Bible, furthermore, God describes himself as a father, and Christ is described as a priest and a king. For many people these are not positive images. Because these images have been distorted, it can be difficult for someone to decide to become either a disciple or a disciplemaker.

But Jesus' view of his authority was not like ours. His view of authority was not about power and oppression, but love and service. After he washed his disciples' feet, he said, "Now that I, your Lord and Teacher, have washed your feet, you also should wash one another's feet" (Jn 13:14). His view of authority was not one of selfishness or success, but of servanthood and humility.

You know that the rulers of the Gentiles lord it over them, and their high officials exercise authority over them. Not so with you. Instead, whoever wants to become great among you must be your servant, and whoever wants to be first must be your slave—just as the Son of Man did not come to be served, but to serve. (Mt 20:25-28)

Jesus' view of authority was not one of manipulation and pressure but that of a host inviting guests to a party (Lk 14:15-24). "Blessed is the man who will eat at the feast in the kingdom of God. . . . Come, for everything is now ready" (vv. 15, 17). It was not a hierarchal view of authority, but one in which he called his followers his friends. "I have called you friends, for everything that I learned from my Father I have made known to you" (Jn 15:15).

As disciplemakers, then, we become servants, hosts and friends to younger Christians. When they have seen Jesus' graciousness and love in us, then they may be ready to hear that the Servant has become King.

Attitudes toward Truth

Jesus' instructions to be disciplemakers have also faded in light of our cultural attitude toward truth.

Philosophically, pluralism has taken over. It is not popular to say that one lifestyle is better than another. We are allowed to disagree with another's point of view, but we are called on by the social milieu of our society to be tolerant and accepting. Pluralism teaches that all persons have a right to their own ideas. No one should try to change what another person thinks. This is done under the guise of "acceptance." Even to some Christians, Christianity is no longer seen as the only correct way to guide our lives. The president of the student body at the American Graduate School of International Management, a young Christian himself, told me: "Since students are here from all over the world, we make a great effort to rise above differences in culture or religion and completely accept everyone." The thread of truth in this perspective carries with it a subtle lie—that there are many "truths," and none that is absolute.

Dr. Allan Bloom, author of *The Closing of the American Mind,* laments the effect of relativism on the college campus. "The danger they have been taught to fear from absolutism, is not error but intolerance."[1] He argues that relativism is destroying the concept of truth. In the name of openness, he says, American minds have been closed.

The kind of thinking Bloom describes challenges the disciplemaker who believes not in many contradictory truths but in *the* Truth, Jesus (Jn 14:6). We dare not buy into relativism. As Christians we cannot accept a diluted view of truth. But how does the Christian student deal with the risk of appearing intolerant and non-accepting in a society where acceptance and tolerance are almost worshiped? How can Christians enthusiastically espouse their faith without looking like fanatics?

I believe the answer to these questions is rooted in our own personal convictions. Do we believe Jesus is who he said he was? Do we believe he meant what he said about lifestyles and value systems? Do we believe that some day in the future his authority will be recognized by everyone?

These are not rhetorical questions. There are times when the answers don't seem clear at all. Sometimes doubt grips my mind. Or fear stains my faith. And sometimes I get so caught up in life that I forget to remember Jesus' claims about truth and authority. At times like these I need to stop and ask myself, "What do I really believe about life and about Jesus?" I find myself responding on at least three different levels: intellectually, emotionally and philosophically.

On an intellectual level, I believe that Jesus' resurrection validates the truth of his teaching. There are many other intellectual arguments which support the truth of Christianity, but it is the resurrection which encourages me the most. In fact, I often go back over the information in the little booklet *The Evidence for the Resurrection* by J. N. D. Anderson (InterVarsity Press). If Jesus did indeed return from death, then all of what he taught must be true.

Emotionally, I find that the experience of true Christian fellowship helps me believe. I have certainly been hurt by counterfeit experiences of fellowship, but for the most part, I have been encouraged by other Christians who love me. In a few significant friendships, I have felt loved with a love which could only come from God. The friends who love me in this way help me believe that Jesus was not only love (1 Jn 4:16) but also truth.

Finally, I am encouraged to believe in Jesus when I look at life philosophically. I have decided that the idea of a personal God makes more sense than the possibility that life came from chaos. (All philosophies have some measure of the unknown. Belief in a personal Creator leaves less unknowns in my mind than other philosophies of life.) If there is a personal God, then it makes sense that he created us for his own reasons. And if a personal God created us for a purpose, then it makes sense that we will operate best when living according to the designer's plan. This is where my intellectual, emotional and philosophical conclusions begin to intersect my disciplemaking efforts.

If, as Scripture says, God created us to have fellowship with him and with each other and to enjoy our surroundings (Gen 1—2), then we are imperfect if we are not living life as he intended we should. Because of our own self-centeredness (rather than God-centeredness), many of us are out of fellowship with God, with each other and with our world. Disciplemakers are not trying to impose an impersonal truth on an unwilling audience. Rather, we are trying to help friends be who they were designed to become.

Essential Truth

Augustine observed that there is a God-shaped vacuum in every heart. In other words, human beings were created to love God. When we are not living in a love relationship to God, we are square pegs in round holes. We are not being who we were created to be and cannot be fully satisfied. We walk around with gaping holes in our hearts.

Remembering this truth will change our attitude toward the society where we are disciplemaking. No matter how loud the political and philosophical voices against the God of Truth, the fact remains that our neighbors and our friends will never find complete satisfaction apart from him.

I was visiting in a home recently when a mockingbird flew uninvited into the basement. As we stood there wondering how to get rid of him, it cowered on the top of a bookcase, looking frightened and out of its element. Birds were created to fly. We look with pity on captive birds or birds with broken wings. Likewise when human beings live their lives outside of fellowship with God, they are frightened, locked in an alien environment.

The difference between our friends and the mockingbird is that human beings teach themselves not to *look* frightened when they are. In fact, we have even taught ourselves to look happy in the captive environment of sin.

We need to remember this perspective if we are going to be disciplemakers. Our friends, Christians and non-Christians, are incomplete and not living life to the fullest if they are not living the lives God created them to live. So when we offer to help them grow in Christ, we are offering satisfaction, wholeness and freedom they will not get elsewhere.

My friend Rosemary and I have been meeting off and on for several years. When we meet, we sometimes look at Scripture and discuss its implications for her life. Sometimes we talk about books. Sometimes we just talk. But our agenda for these times is to focus on Rosemary and her growth as a believer in Jesus. It is a temptation for me to feel presumptuous and impertinent to think that I could be Rosemary's spiritual guide or mentor. But our times together have, in fact, helped Rosemary grow.

She recently expressed her frustration at not being able to get beyond a sense of ignorance and inability. "God has gifted lots of other people," she told me. "But I really don't see any spiritual gifts that I have."

"You know, Rosemary," I suggested, "I think you may have the gift of evangelism."

"What? You've got to be kidding!" she replied, astonished.

She could hardly believe what I was saying. But I reminded her of several instances when she helped non-Christians learn more about Jesus. I could see a light go on in her brain. Rosemary left that day with a little more eagerness and confidence in how God was using her.

The next week, Rosemary was flying high with stories of how she had shared her faith with others. Our conversation had helped her discover another facet of the person God had created her to be. She found her spiritual wings, and they worked! Since then we have continued to discuss the conversations she has with friends. In spite of my fears of presumption, as I help Rosemary grow, I have a sense of polishing a beautiful gift from God. Again and again I have seen that this kind of involvement helps people to find and to enjoy the place God has for them.

Disciplemaking, then, flies in the face of a society which says that we should not interfere in others' lives, that we have nothing to offer anyone which is better than what they could discover on their own. Disciplemaking offers truth and authority to a society which secretly longs for both. Disciplemakers help people become all they were meant to be.

Notes

[1]Allan Bloom, *The Closing of the American Mind* (New York: Simon & Schuster, 1987), p. 25.

Putting It All Together

1. To what extent do you agree or disagree with the suggestion on some bumper stickers to "Question Authority"?

2. As a child growing up, what were some of your experiences with authority in your home?

In your church?

In your school?

How have these experiences influenced your understanding of Jesus' claim to be teacher and Lord (Jn 13:13)?

3. Imagine someone asked you the famous philosophical question "What is truth?" How would you answer?

4. When you picture yourself discipling another person, what feelings arise within you?

5. Describe several ways that being a Christian has helped you discover more about who you were created to be.

6. Look at 1 Timothy 1:3-5.

What "myths" and "false doctrines" are most popular in your circle of friends?

What would be some effective ways to redirect people from false doctrines to truth?

Paul wrote, "The goal of this command is love" (v. 5). How can you "command" and "love" at the same time?

6
FEAR: BEYOND PERSONAL OBSTACLES

As we look further at the reasons why it is hard to obey Jesus' instructions to be disciplemakers, we must be honest enough to look inside ourselves as well as inside our society. In fact, for many of us the greatest obstacles come from within. Many of us bear a scarlet letter, not the large A of Hawthorne's heroine, but the large F of *Fear*.

The world is full of Christians who are friends to both believers and non-believers. Many of these Christian people are living lives that others long to understand and experience themselves. But instead of extending an invitation to the feast, many well-meaning Christians abort the work of God in their lives and in the lives of their friends.

This tragedy occurs when we learn, we grow, we change, but we do not reproduce. Is it possible that at the moment when Jesus wants to use us to accomplish his work on earth, we desert him in fear, just as the early disciples did? (Mt 26:15). Unfortunately, we know that this is not only possible, but true; we have, in fact, deserted Jesus in the disciplemaking process.

When I consider with sadness my own desertions, when I look at the large F on my chest, I see that I have often given in to the fear of rejection and the fear of failure. I am afraid of what others will think of me, and I am afraid that if I stick my neck out, I might fall flat on my face.

I am afraid that others will think I am pushy at best and a fanatic at worst. I am afraid they will think I am patronizing because I want to help them. I am afraid they will like me less when they find out I want to see them grow in Christ. I am afraid, to my own shame, that my popularity will wane.

And truthfully, we may not be popular if we talk about the sovereignty and authority of Jesus. But Jesus himself didn't win any popularity contests (unless you count the Homecoming Parade into Jerusalem on Palm Sunday). Jesus "had no beauty or majesty to attract us to him, nothing in his appearance that we should desire him. He was despised and rejected by men" (Is 53:2-3). If popularity and acceptance are our goals, then we need to evaluate those goals in light of Jesus' example. Scripture does not teach us to be popular, tolerant and loved by our peers. Rather, we are to be faithful, truthful and loving.

But God is good. He does not ask many of us to suffer the pain of rejection as we seek to love our friends and to make disciples. When the fear of rejection begins to grip us, we need to stop and do a "reality check." How often, in fact, have we been rejected because we reached out to someone? How often has someone taken offense when we offered to pray for them or to study Scripture with them? Perhaps we have been turned down because of lack of interest. But my guess is that our efforts have rarely, if ever, been unappreciated. Most people, even if they do not verbalize it, appreciate someone caring about them enough to want to spend time with them to help them grow in their faith. The friends I have reached out to, whose lives I have touched, have confirmed my own experience: When I am hiding, I want to be found, and I welcome the loving arms that look for me.

Our attitudes, furthermore, make a large difference. To borrow from an old expression, disciplemaking is a situation where one beggar tells another beggar where to find food. If you do not look down, your friend will not need to look up. If you do not seek to be admired, your friend will not need to revere. If you share your own needs and weaknesses, your friend will be freer to share his.

Something to Tell

The apostle Paul used an analogy which gives further help. He wrote that we are to be people with secrets. "Men ought to regard us as servants of Christ and as those entrusted with the secret things of God" (1 Cor 4:1). Do your friends look at you as someone with secrets to tell? I can still remember being a six-year-old and running into the closet with a friend so we could share our secrets away from the ears of my parents. What excitement I felt that she would tell me her secrets and that I could tell her mine!

There are people all around us who want to know our secrets. They aren't squealing with eagerness like two children hiding in a closet, but they are dying to know, nevertheless. After several decades of being a Christian, I still want to know the secrets of the friends I admire. I learn from others daily and will for the rest of my life.

If you begin to behave as though you have secrets which will change peoples lives, I can almost guarantee that you will find others who want what you have to offer. One of the effects of our society's reluctance to reach out to others is a tremendous need for direction. People long for values but do not know which direction to turn in order to find guidance. Allan Bloom observed that today's students are "flat-souled."[1] People all around us are crying silently for help.

And still our fear may keep us from being bold and loving in reaching out to them. The scarlet *F* also stands for *Fear of failure*. And this fear is, indeed, rooted in reality. I know I have failed many times. But this is no surprise to God. Actually, while I might see my fear of failure as a liability, I have learned that it can also be God's gift to me to remind me that I am not self-sufficient.

Fruit in Spite of Fear

One of the privileges of being in the discipleship business for many years is that time proves that God is sovereign and that he is greater than my fears and my failures. I often receive letters from students I knew ten or twenty years ago. "Thank you," some write. "You helped me grow as a Christian." Often they tell me that they are now missionaries, parents, doctors, professors or active church members. Sometimes I laugh at the cosmic joke. For often these relationships were the very ones where I thought I had failed. And perhaps I did fail—but God did not.

One of my friends, Jason, is an InterVarsity staff member in the Midwest. He told me about one of his "failures." He was visiting Lee, a student at a campus he visited once a month. Jason initiated a Bible study with Lee in the book of Titus. But Lee was distracted and continued to direct the conversation to other things. Jason was sure nothing had been accomplished.

But the joke was on him. When Jason visited the campus the following month, he discovered that Lee had been so excited about their Bible study in Titus that he had already shared the study with three other students.

Our perception of success and failure may, in fact, be inaccurate. When we think we fail, we need to question ourselves about whether or not God is trying to teach us something through a sense of failure. If we cannot think of anything we should change, then we need to question whether or not our sense of failure is accurate. Perhaps the almighty God has chosen to work through us without letting us know. We may find out years later that what we saw as failure was actually God's success.

Fear in disciplemaking is not limited to twentieth-century Christians. Timothy, one of the first disciplemakers, apparently had a problem with fear. Paul, Timothy's own discipler, had to remind him not to be afraid. To Timothy he wrote, "God did not give us a spirit of timidity, but a spirit of power, of love and of self-discipline" (2 Tim 1:7). It is interesting to speculate whether or not it was Timothy's young age which caused him to fear. In an earlier letter Paul had written, "Don't let anyone look down on you because you are young, but set an example for the believers in speech, in life, in love, in faith and in purity" (1 Tim 4:12).

When I look back over the years, I smile at some of the things I was afraid of as a youth. The fears were real, but now I know they represented phantoms. I have never arrived at a stage in life where I am not afraid of anything, but the sources of fear have changed. Paul reached out and reassured Timothy at just the spot where he needed it. That his concern for Timothy ran deep is evidenced by his request to the Corinthian church: "If Timothy comes, see to it that he has nothing to fear while he is with you, for he is carrying on the work of the Lord, just as I am. No one, then, should refuse to accept him" (1 Cor 16:10-11). Neither does God condemn us for our fear. He reassures us and helps us.

God's Fools

In my own fears, I am reassured and helped by Paul's reminder that "the foolishness of God is wiser than man's wisdom, and the weakness of God is stronger than man's strength. . . . Not many of you were wise by human standards; not many were influential; not many were of noble birth. But God chose the foolish things of the world to shame the wise; God chose the weak things of the world to shame the strong" (1 Cor 1:25-27).

Several years ago I saw an advertisement for an oil-painting class:

Make-It Take-It Painting Workshop
You never have to have held a paintbrush in your hand.

"Well, I qualify," I said to myself as I signed up for the class. God also takes novices, foolish people, simple people and weak people to be disciplemakers. I qualify for that too. And my experience has been that these very qualities of foolishness, simplicity and weakness do, in fact, allow me to see God at work way beyond anything I could do myself.

But I sometimes still wish I had a little pill I could take to banish my fears of rejection and failure. But no pill will ever do the trick. Only one thing will help: experience. I never overcome my fear by standing on the sidelines. Likewise, you will have to jump in to find out that disciplemaking is one of the most rewarding experiences a Christian can have. It's worth ignoring your fears and taking the plunge.

Disciplemaking has a price tag. It takes time, energy and courage. It takes time to live in a discipling friendship. It takes emotional energy to overcome fear and to buck the tide of societal norms. It takes courage to be known, to reach out in spite of our fears and to risk the possibility that success may not be obvious to us.

Because of this cost, I sometimes wonder why Jesus chose us for the task. Maybe he should have used stones to declare his glory after all (Mt 3:9). But until I see stones walking around and discipling people, I will assume that God thinks people like us are more suited to the task. Perhaps this is for our own good. Perhaps it is so that he will receive the credit. Or perhaps it is because it is his nature to reach out in love, to draw people to himself and, because we are created in his image, he wants us to be imitators of him.

Notes

[1]Allan Bloom, *The Closing of the American Mind* (New York: Simon & Schuster, 1987), p. 134.

Putting It All Together

1. The fear of rejection and the fear of failure are two obstacles in disciplemaking. Which of these fears or what other fear do you experience most frequently in relationships?

When was the last time you held back from a relationship because of this fear?

2. Jeremiah 42:11 reads: "Do not be afraid of the king of Babylon, whom you now fear. Do not be afraid of him, declares the LORD, for I am with you and will save you and deliver you from his hands."

Rewrite this verse, filling in the blanks with words that describe your life and God's promise to you.

Do not be afraid of _____ whom you now fear.

Do not be afraid of _____ , declares the Lord, for _____ .

3. Sometimes in dealing with fear, it helps to look at times when other people have been afraid of us. Think of a time when someone was afraid of you. Describe the situation. What were your thoughts and feeling about that person at that time?

4. Courage is not the absence of fear. It is acting in spite of the fear. List the courageous steps you need to take in order to disciple someone.

What will help you take these steps?

5. Make a list of reasons why you want to move ahead as a disciplemaker in spite of any fears you may have.

SECTION 2
PRACTICING
DISCIPLEMAKING

7

HOW TO BE
A FRIEND

J im, Jeanette, Sue, Bill. *These peo-
ple* were not just would-be disciples. They were, first of all,
friends. Just as discipleship is a relationship with Jesus, so disciplemaking is a relationship between two friends. And being a
friend is not something everyone knows how to do. Some who
want to learn to be disciplemakers need first of all to learn how
to be friends.

There is an epidemic of self-absorption in our society. This
epidemic is not rooted in something bad but in something good.
Awareness of individual preferences, making provision to have
our own needs met, is good for our health. But the danger of this
awareness is preoccupation with self. There are some who say
that we've come a long way: now we know how to "look out for
number one." Others see in the phenomenon the seed of relational alienation in our culture.

We have, indeed, "come a long way." It is certainly positive that many of us have learned to be self-aware, confident and appropriately assertive. This is something that our generation has worked hard to learn. But there is a dark side to this strength. Just as Samson's physical strength brought about his own death, so it is that good in excess becomes evil. Eating, drinking and sex are good things which, when taken to sinful extremes, become gluttony, drunkenness and sexual immorality. In a similar but more subtle way, our self-awareness may lead to self-absorption and self-preoccupation.

I notice this often when I am at social gatherings. After spending two or three hours with friends, I sometimes leave with a sense of sadness. Many times I relate this sadness to the fact that no one asked me anything about myself. No one seemed to want to know about me, my interests and activities. No one reached out to touch me with a personal word of encouragement or a loving question.

I do not think this is because people really do not want to reach out. I think it is because they do not know how. Whatever the merits of our heightened consciousness of self, few can refute that one risk of self-consciousness is an atrophied ability to reach out to others. I sometimes think that if our society were to be pictured symbolically on film, we might choose millions of dots, each with many fast-moving, concentric circles surrounding it. They bump into each other, to be sure, but they rarely penetrate each other's spheres. Our lives, sad to say, revolve around ourselves.

This was certainly not Jesus' pattern. Nor can it be ours if we want to be disciplemakers. Indeed the very first step in making a disciple is to reach out and care for a friend. But because we live in a self-absorbed world, we have much to learn about befriending each other and caring, as Jesus cared, for one another's needs.

Since this is a critical part of disciplemaking, I would like to suggest several skills that have helped me in building relationships: looking through another's eyes, being curious, asking questions, practicing hospitality, laughing together and praying together.

Looking through Another's Eyes

The first skill is the ability to see life through others' eyes. When I look through others' eyes, I see their lives as they see them. It does not mean I agree with them. Acceptance is not necessarily approval. But it does mean that I have taken the time to try to see what they see.

I had a conversation recently with someone who was accused of immorality. Now I do not approve of sexual sin. But as my friend talked I tried to see what she saw. She did not think she was guilty of the immorality she was accused of committing. She felt that she was the victim of a harsh and unforgiving criticism. Whether she was guilty of sexual sin or not, I could "accept" the fact that harsh criticism and an unforgiving spirit are painful attitudes to face. If we had had occasion to talk longer, we might have dealt with whether or not her actions really were sinful. But at first, I needed to understand her sense that she had been unjustly condemned.

One facet of seeing life through someone else's eyes is the appreciation of human differences. I have always heard that no two snowflakes look alike, and I have accepted that on faith. (I've never had the inclination to check out every snowflake that lands in my front yard.) It is easier for me to believe that no two flowers are exactly alike, because I have compared different roses on the same bush and various marigolds in the window box. And the longer I observe human nature, the more convinced I am that no two people ever respond in exactly the same way to the same situation. You may be afraid of mountain climbing, and I may be afraid of mountain climbing, but our fears are different. You may like to go to church, and I may like to go to church, but that does not mean we both like church in the same way.

For this reason, an expression like "I know just how you feel" makes little sense when you are building a loving relationship. When I was sick for three months with a virus similar to mononucleosis, many well-meaning people tried to comfort me by saying, "Oh, I know just how you feel. I had a cold last month." I wanted to shout to the world, "You do not know how I feel! You do not have my body and you do not know how my mind responds to what my body is doing!" I wanted people to *ask* me about my experience and to take a moment to look at life through my eyes. Reaching out to others includes allowing them to speak about their experiences in their own words.

Sometimes this means looking beneath the facts in order to understand another's experience. I recently hurt a friend by offering to do something for her she wanted done. I followed through on my promise with good intentions, but my heart wasn't in it. I pretended to be happy to do as she asked. But as it turned out, she realized that I did not want to be with her then, and she was very hurt. In fact, her hurt became a challenge to our relationship.

I wanted to defend myself. "But you shouldn't take it that way! I was only trying to please you." I wanted her not to be hurt. I thought her hurt was unfounded. But the more I resisted her pain, the more tense the relationship became. The more I defended myself, the more she defended herself. Our friendship was being squeezed by the jugular.

Finally, I let go of my half. I did it by looking at the situation through her eyes. She was hurt. She felt that I had lied to her. I didn't think I had. But the experience of being lied to does hurt. I could understand that. So I apologized.

It was only when I could get underneath very trivial circumstances and see that my friend was dealing with issues of truth and falseness that our relationship could be restored.

Jesus was very good at seeing things through another's eyes and acknowledging each person's unique experiences. When he healed the woman with the flow of blood in Mark 5, he did it publicly. Looking at the situation through only my own eyes, I thought it unkind and embarrassing to publicly point out the woman's healing of a very private illness. But Jesus knew that the woman had not just had been menstruating for twelve years. She had also been ceremonially unclean according to Jewish law. That meant that she would have been shunned by her community. Jesus knew that this private illness had to be dealt with publicly in order to restore the woman, not just physically but also socially and culturally. Jesus saw the woman's needs as she must have seen them herself.

Being Curious
Learning to look at life through another's eyes requires curiosity. The dot spheres on my imaginary movie screen bump into each other, but they are not curious about those interactions. Their concentric circles keep them from being interested in anyone other than themselves. But what a gift curiosity is! My friend has it. She asks me many questions about myself. She is genuinely interested in me and even asks me about some of the trivia in my life. And she asks me about my feelings, my spiritual growth and my current intellectual pursuits. I am always sure of her interest in me—and sure that she is a friend.

Curiosity is not so much a skill to be learned as it is an art to be practiced. Practice becoming aware of what interests you about other people. Practice setting aside your own assumptions. Practice asking for other people's ideas. Practice curiosity.

The summer I was sick, I had more than one person say to me, "I'd ask you how you feel, but I'm sure you don't want to talk about it." I was tempted to yell, "Wait a minute! Hold your horses! I *do* want to talk about it! In fact there is nothing I'd rather talk about right now!" The people who made those comments may have wanted to be helpful, but they were actually making a false assumption about me which squelched their own curiosity and my ability to talk about my experience.

Most people want to talk about themselves. Some people, of course, are quite shy. And when we reach out to people, we are not to do it with emotional can openers, prying for secrets and intimacies. But almost everyone likes to be asked about something. One of our jobs in loving others is to find out what they like to talk about and then engage them in conversation on that topic. An excellent way to get to know someone is to ask about things that really excite the person.

Asking Questions

The ability to ask good questions is a skill which is often untapped. In our society it is more common to hear people talking about themselves than asking questions of others. Self-absorbed people do not ask questions. If you are out of practice, if your capacity to ask loving questions has atrophied, here are some reminders: good questions are honest, appropriate and open-ended.

First of all, ask about things which honestly interest you. I do not ask my friends if they watched yesterday's football game on TV because I am not as interested in sports as I am in other things. I don't ask what someone had for breakfast because I rarely care. But I have yet to meet anyone who did not give some hint about something of personal interest that I was also interested in. When I get that hint, I zero in, asking the person to tell me more.

Sometimes this is tricky. I remember standing in line beside someone at a conference, waiting for lunch, and I wanted to reach out to her. But after I learned the woman's name, I could not for the life of me think of how to get a conversation started. So I said what I was thinking, which was a question: "What should I ask you about yourself to help me get to know you a little?" She jumped right in and started telling me her life history.

The wonderful thing about questions is that they give you the opportunity to focus on a topic that is of genuine interest to you. And they give your friends the opportunity to respond on the level they choose. They also give your friends the opportunity to be known, one of the main ingredients of love.

Second, ask questions which are appropriate to the level of friendship you have with someone. This does not necessarily mean how long you have known a person. Appropriateness has more to do with a sense of comradery or kinship. I had someone I'd known only a few days ask me, "What is your passion in life?" I did not mind such a personal question because the person who asked it was obviously genuinely interested in my answer and was someone who had quickly won my respect. On the other hand, I have resisted such a simple question as, "What did you learn from the sermon today?" because the person inquiring seemed to be asking mechanically and without real interest. When that happens I do not feel free to share personal thoughts, struggles or joys.

It is not always easy to tell ahead of time whether or not a question is appropriate. Sometimes I ask a preceding question, "Do you mind my asking you about your surgery? or your quiet time? or our friendship?" The idea behind a good question is: "I would like to look at this topic the way you look at it. This will help me get to know you better, and it will help me understand the topic more." When this is the attitude behind the question, it is more likely to find its proper level of appropriateness.

Finally, ask open-ended questions. Do not ask "loaded" questions which are seeking predetermined answers. Invite opinions different from your own. If, for example, a woman you know is dating a non-Christian, you could ask, "How is it going with John? Do you think he is helping or hurting your spiritual life?" But, beware! Your friend may say, "Oh, he's helping! I'm learning to trust God on my own, without the help of Christian friends." Then you might ask, "Oh, what things are you learning?" As you listen to the reply, you are looking at the relationship through your friend's eyes. After taking a good look, you might ask, "Do you think you could have learned those things in any other way?" or "How is your experience preparing you for Christian marriage?" or "Do you have concerns about dating a non-Christian?"

So far, you may feel that you have done nothing to convince your friend that dating non-Christians is a stupid thing to do, but in fact you have gotten the wheels moving. God the Holy Spirit convinces men and women of sin, and he will be working in your friend's thoughts as she answers.

The Spirit might urge you on. You might ask, "Would you like to talk about Ephesians 5:21-33 together sometime to see what God says about marriage?" or "Do you mind if I share what happened to me when I dated a non-Christian?"

All of these questions may seem slow and cumbersome but think what would have happened if you had started out with, "Do you know why God doesn't want you to date a non-Christian?" *Slam.* End of conversation.

Perhaps these questions seem manipulative. This is an appropriate caution. Questions can be manipulative. But they will be only if your intention is to manipulate. They will not be if you are genuinely interested in your friend, open in your love and very willing to the response.

Practicing Hospitality
Another skill which we can develop to build better relationships is the skill of hospitality. My experience with hospitality is

that it comes in three forms: extensive sharing of your home and life, entertaining visitors and relational hospitality.

The first kind of hospitality is the kind that my friends Joanne and Julie practice. They regularly invite people to stay in their apartment for extended periods of time. Their home is a drop-in spot for students who live nearby. Their dinner table always has room for one more. Extensive hospitality like this is indeed a gift of the Spirit.

The second form of hospitality is probably the most familiar to us. It is the invitation-to-dinner kind of hospitality. We give to our guests not just a meal but the experience of a pleasant time in our home. This kind of hospitality is important as a building block in relationships, but it should not become the end of our hospitable efforts. In fact, I would be hard put to say that entertaining is biblical hospitality in the truest sense of the word. I think Jesus would have said that returning the invitation for dinner is a nice thing to do but not really God's idea of love and hospitality (Lk 6:33).

Hospitality, finally, is a welcoming of someone into your life and into your heart and mind. Even without physical touch, it is an embracing with words and curiosity that touch another's heart. I often try to extend hospitality to waitresses and sales-clerks by taking a moment to ask them something about their work. I extend hospitality to my friend by calling and saying, "I just wanted to know what your day is like." And, of course, some-times I extend hospitality in my home with a meal or a cup of tea.

But it is deceptive to think that just because someone is in my home I am being hospitable in the relational sense. During a weekend conference once, I was assigned housing with a Christian family in the area. I happened to stay with them on the night of their favorite TV show. From the time I arrived until I went to bed, we watched television. They may have thought they were being hospitable by housing me during the conference, but in fact what they gave me was merely bed and board.

To understand the fullest meaning of hospitality, think of life as being made up of hosts and guests. The hosts of life are the ones who are available to listen, who offer compassion by being genuine and honest about themselves and who invite you to feel at home, wherever you are. The guests are those who respond. They are the ones who receive acceptance, peace, stimulation and love from the hosts.

We all take turns being hosts and guests. But if we are going to be disciplemakers, we need to realize that the burden of invitation will usually be on us. The New Testament admonitions to practice hospitality (1 Pet 4:9; Rom 12:13; 1 Tim 3:2) mean that we need to be opening up our lives, our hearts and our minds—as well as our homes—to those who want to follow Jesus.

Laughing Together

Lest disciplemaking friendships begin to sound like all work and no play, let me quickly add that hospitality also involves having fun together. Some of us who are serious disciplemakers need to learn to let down our hair, to share the less serious sides of ourselves, to laugh with our young Christian friends. Games, days off, even fun work projects, all build intimacy into relationships.

Laughter is part of the glue that cements a friendship. When I met my new friend, Sharon, we discovered we had much in common. We liked the same kinds of books; we shared many similar values; our goals in life were parallel. We even had several mutual friends. So far, so good—but we were so serious!

Then one evening we started talking about the silly things we do in the security of our closest relationships. Sharon mimics beer commercials. I talk like a dog. As we laughed together, at each other and with each other, our friendship was sealed. Laughter did what serious talk had only begun.

Praying Together

The last skill I want to mention for building relationships is the skill of prayer. We dare not see through another's eyes, ask questions or extend hospitality if we are not also praying. In building discipling relationships, or any kind of friendships, it is not that we are doing great things for God. It is that God is at work, and we may have the privilege of coming alongside and affirming some of his work. When we are praying, our relationships are not "projects" to do but people to love.

Learning to pray for our friends requires realistic expectations. When I went to summer camp as a child, I learned the little song "Make new friends, but keep the old. One is silver and the other gold." For a long time that must have been the motto for my prayer life. I kept voluminous lists of people I wanted to pray for. The problem was that my lists were so long that I knew I couldn't finish them. So more often than not, I decided not to begin.

I've since discovered that one of the most helpful things in my prayer life is to keep my lists short. Every month or two I revise my short list. Some names, those I am closest to, are always on my list. Others are on for several months. Sometimes I just pray for a friend every day for one month. I believe God causes my life to intersect other lives for his purposes and in his timing. I pray with that perspective.

Just yesterday I added Barbara to my prayer list. She is someone I've known for a long time, but I just learned that she is very discouraged. I want to go and tell her that it's foolishness for someone with her talent to feel like a failure. But I haven't looked at life yet through her eyes. I want to ask her to tell me about what she is experiencing, but I haven't seen her to ask her. I want to invite her into my emotional and spiritual space and try to be supportive of her. I don't know whether she will accept the invitation or not. But I decided that I will pray, every day, that God the Holy Spirit will comfort her and encourage her, help her to see her life truthfully, accepting both her strengths and weaknesses. God is already at work in Barbara's life. If my life touches her life soon, God may use me as a vehicle for his work. If not, I'll be a closet disciplemaker, praying for Barbara as long as God gives me concern for her.

All of these friendship-building activities require tremendous involvement and commitment. It takes love and grace to see through another's eyes, to be curious, to ask questions, to be hospitable, to pray. But these activities are not just prerequisites to disciplemaking. Being a friend is more than the beginning. It is at the heart of the whole disciplemaking process.

Putting It All Together
1. Write a definition of *friend*.
Jesus said, "I have called you friends" (Jn 15:15). In light of your definition of a friend, write down at least three ways Jesus befriended his disciples.
Who are you a friend to?
2. This chapter describes five qualities of friendship. Think about the friends in your life right now. Fill in the chart on page 83 to remind yourself how you can develop your friendship skills further.
3. List questions you wish people had asked you this week.
Make a list of generic questions which interest you and you would like to ask other people as the occasions arise.
4. What kind of hospitality do you enjoy receiving the most?
What kind of hospitality do you enjoy giving the most?
In what ways would you like to improve your hospitality?
5. Make a short list of people you would like to pray for this week.

Quality	Name of friend	How will I demonstrate this quality with my friend?
Looking at life through another's eyes		
Asking questions		
Hospitality		
Prayer		

Resource on Being a Friend

How Can I Ask Good Questions?

1. *Ask open-ended questions.* Avoid yes and no questions. Ask, "What do you like about living in New Mexico?" rather than, "Do you like living in New Mexico?"

2. In casual, social situations, *ask easy questions.* Ask for biographical data: "Do you have a job? Do you have children? What's your major?" Ask, "What do you do in your free time?" You can even ask, "What kinds of things do you enjoy talking about?"

3. *Be curious.* Look for an area where your friend knows more than you. "What's it like to take twenty credits? or to be married to a politician? or to have seven brothers and sisters?" "What has surprised you about college? about marriage? about living here?"

Ask about experiences your friend has had that you haven't had. "I can't imagine going to the same college my mother went to. What is that like?" "I can't imagine losing someone so close to me. How has that been for you?"

4. *Ask about what really interests you.* If you don't want to hear the answer, don't ask the question.

5. *Ask if a question is appropriate* if you are not sure. Say, "Would you mind if I asked you what you do for your quiet time?"

6. *Remember that asking why can be threatening.* Instead of asking, "Why do you feel that way?" ask, "Would you tell me more about how you feel?"

7. *Don't manipulate.* If you know someone is having trouble praying, don't try to remind him to pray by asking, "What did you ask God for today?" Instead, ask about his concerns and then volunteer, "How would you feel if I prayed with you about these things?"

8. *Ask questions with your eyes as well as your mouth.* If you are looking over your friend's left shoulder as you ask important questions, your conversation will fall flat no matter how good your questions are.

9. *Try to find out what your friend wants to talk about.* "What things would you like to tell me about your trip?" "What are some of the things you are thinking about these days?" "What's your favorite question to be asked?"

8
HOW TO ESTABLISH A DISCIPLING RELATIONSHIP

Most of us have an abundance of friends—and as Christians, these friendships will be with non-Christian friends as well as Christian friends. We are, of course, to reach out to our non-Christian friends with the love of Jesus. But what about our Christian friends? How does God want us to reach out to them?

The Christian friends we have are either growing in their faith, stagnant or someplace in between. Disciplemakers look around at their circle of friends and are drawn to help them grow. Friends who are already growing may need refinement and polishing, because a Christian never outgrows the need for encouragement. But the Christian friends who are stagnant or in a slow cooker may need more than that. They may need an invitation to enter into the serious business of Christian growth.

If you feel drawn to a Christian friend and want to offer to disciple that person, do it. Don't let anyone stop you. It is at this point, when we are drawn to reach out to a friend, that the Enemy of the faith challenges us and tries to abort our efforts. It may be through our personal fears, societal pressures or even circumstances. But the most effective way to fight the Enemy is to jump right into the battle.

Reach out to your friend. Make arrangements to have a meal together. Get to know the person better. Find out what your friend's interests are. Let the person get to know you. Then if you see the friendship deepening, take the all-important step of asking if your friend would like to get together with you to try a six-week, three-month or semester-long, custom-made discipleship program.

Making this question definite does two important things. It gives you permission to enter more deeply into your friend's life, thus taking a significant step to overcome many of the obstacles in the disciplemaking process, and it defines the relationship so that it becomes more effective for Christian growth than a simple friendship would be.

Most Christians have never experienced a discipling relationship like this, so this will be a new experience. This means that we have to take the initiative. It means that we have to reach out in friendship. And it means that we have to take the risk of defining the discipleship process.

Establishing a Relationship

Many of the people we seek to disciple will already be our friends. If not, then the first thing you must do is to become friends. This is what I needed to do with Maria. When we first met I knew Maria's mother, but I did not know Maria, a junior in college. Maria was a committed Christian but on the fringes of the college group at church. She wanted to use her gifts to serve God, but she was in a fog about how to do that. Rather than rush in with my bright headlights on (they just reflect back the fog anyway), I first took time to get to know Maria.

I found out that she was the youngest of seven children and had close relationships with several brothers and sisters. By inviting her to tell me what it was like to be the youngest of seven, she became the expert, and we were off. For the next hour and several cups of coffee, we laughed over numerous stories and traced the trails of six older siblings. I shared from my own family experience so Maria would begin to know me as well.

During this special time of getting to know her family and what she enjoyed doing, I also wanted to learn about Maria's spiritual pilgrimage. She told me about her high-school years and her first two years in college, leading to where she was at the time. She told me about one really good year in high school and about what made it important in her life. She told me about her college group at church and what turned her off about that.

Then she told me about the fog. She didn't know what to do with her Christian life, her gifts, her lack of Christian friends. She didn't know where to begin, what to do or who could help. All of this was expressed indirectly as she described her recent spiritual journey and lack of involvement in a support group.

Then I asked Maria if she would like to meet together in a discipling relationship. I was surprised at her eagerness. We began to explore places where we could begin. I asked her first if she was having a daily time in Scripture and what she was doing. This is the key place to begin to grow spiritually, but my experience has told me that few believers have had helpful training so that they know how to dig into Scripture on their own.

Then my questions focused around Maria's concerns. Was there an area in her Christian life or an area of struggle which she wanted to focus on? Perhaps we could develop Bible study skills by doing a study on her area of interest. Or was there a book she'd like to read and discuss? What were her most urgent questions about her faith? What were the issues she struggled with most often? Together we tried to define the needs that our times together might speak to.

This is how I started a discipling relationship with Maria, but you may begin the process quite differently. It took me a while to get to know Maria. You probably also have some people in your life you already know who are at various places in their growth as Christians. For some of those friends, your discipling efforts will focus on shared experiences, where your life and influence rub off on them. But in some friendships, there is opportunity for a more specific kind of disciplemaking. There are probably one or two Christians in your life right now who would like to have you help them grow. Pray that God will lead you to them.

Plan Ahead

The next step in establishing a discipling relationship is often overlooked: it is essential to establish a plan. A plan not only sets the agenda for your times together, it also gives you both permission and motivation to be persistent in your efforts. In addition, following a plan is following the example of our Lord.

God is a Person with a plan. From Genesis through Revelation, we see the working out of God's plan to bring all men to himself. In Psalm 139 we see that he also has a plan for each individual life. "All the days ordained for me were written in your book before one of them came to be" (Ps 139:16). Jesus had a plan for his disciples when he called them and sent them out two by two (Mt 10:1-15). The plans we make for a discipling relationship merely imitate the kind of carefulness God has for his work.

The plan for a discipling relationship must be growth-centered, not program-centered. This means that the desires and needs of the person you are discipling have a major part in determining what you do together. It also means that your own learning style and teaching style will be considered. (Learning styles will be discussed in more detail in chapter ten.) You and your friend may like having a very definite outline of where you are going. Or you may prefer to be more open-ended and flow with needs as they arise. What is important is that you avoid the two extremes of no plan at all and a plan so rigid that it fails to adjust to current issues.

As you talk with your friend about what you want your times together to be like, take the initiative to offer several alternatives based on the specific individual. If you have been in a discipling relationship before, do not assume that what was meaningful in that situation will be in this one. This is why it is so important to take sufficient time to get to know the person. We know that people are not carbon copies. There are similarities for sure. But everyone is unique, and our plans must reflect their uniqueness if we are to be effective.

The plan must also allow for periodic times of evaluation. How helpful has it been? Is it hitting the target areas? Should the plan be altered in any way? This shows your commitment to be a true servant to your friend.

A plan for a discipling relationship should have six key components: topic, material, logistics, method, evaluation and reproduction. For instance, your topic may be prayer, how to know God's will or some other growth area. Your material may be a Bible-study guide, a book or some other means to zero in on your topic. Logistics include when and where you will meet, how long each meeting will last, and for how many weeks or months you will meet. How will you use your time together? Will you include time for personal sharing? Time for Bible study? Time for prayer? Will you have time simply to have fun together and share relaxing experiences? When will you take stock and evaluate whether or not you are heading where you intended? What can you do to help your friend also become a disciplemaker? How can you encourage him "to teach others" also (2 Tim 2:2)?

The resource section of this chapter, and following chapters give ideas for plans in discipling relationships.

Do you realize what a plan like this communicates to your friend? You are saying, "I love you enough to give you hours of my life, devoting my attention to your concerns and giving my energy to help you grow." Certainly, this reflects Jesus' words: "Greater love has no one than this, that he lay down his life for his friends" (Jn 15:13).

Detours

One benefit of having a plan is that it will guide you to where you are going. But one of the tensions of having a plan is that there are times when you need to set it aside. It is possible that your well-intended plan may occasionally interfere with meeting immediate, urgent needs.

This happened with Maria and me. During the weeks we were meeting, her family sold their home, and Maria got a new job. Both these changes were traumatic for Maria. Because of them, we missed two meetings together. When we met the next time, I suggested we set aside our planned book study and talk about her recent experiences. We centered our discussion around biblical truths that would comfort her and encourage her to remember that God is trustworthy.

We need to beware of detours offered by Satan to get us off the track, but we need to be sensitive to God's work and any new paths he may introduce into our plan. "In his heart a man plans his course, but the LORD determines his steps" (Prov 16:9).

The environment for a healthy discipling relationship, then, is flexible, open and person-centered. Together, you and your friend are assuming that God is actively at work in your lives.

We need to help our friends recognize and define what God is doing in their lives. We must honestly share in our friends' struggles and efforts to respond to God. This will often mean cheering them on and erecting the milestones to their growth. At the same time, we need to provide input for more growth. All the while, we will be growing too but the emphasis in these relationships will be on our friends' growth. We are the initiators, finding the paths for our friends—out of the bushes, into the garden, where God will give them many good gifts.

Putting It All Together
1. From the list below, check the ways you feel about the ideas presented in this chapter regarding planning.
_____ frustrated _____ confused _____ resistant _____ anxious
_____ eager _____ guilty _____ suspicious _____ in agreement
Why do you think you feel this way?
How might your feelings in this area affect your personal experience in disciplemaking?
2. List each idea in this chapter regarding discipleship which is new for you.
If you apply this new information to your life, how will that affect your efforts at disciplemaking?
3. What hesitations do you have about establishing a defined discipling relationship? List them.
Show your list to a trusted friend. Ask for feedback as to which ones are real problems to be solved and which ones are imagined problems to be ignored.
4. Read Proverbs 16:3, 9. How do you think these verses apply to a discipling relationship?

Resource for Establishing a Discipling Relationship

Checklist for Finding a Friend to Disciple
The following steps summarize the things you can do to find a person to disciple, to initiate a relationship with the person and to define your discipleship plan.

1. Look at yourself first and see if you are communicating an open, accepting attitude. People are interested in a one-to-one relationship when:

    a. They know we will deal with their perceived needs first rather than our own agendas for them.

    b. They know we will be people-centered in approach, not program-centered.

    c. We create a warm atmosphere of hospitality and care for them.

    d. They perceive us as learners with them and not as the "experts."

    e. When we are willing to be flexible in our goals, but also prepared to teach them something.

2. If you are open to others and eager for God to use you, then you can begin to look for someone to disciple by:

    a. Praying that God will lead you to someone who needs what you have to offer.

    b. Keeping your eyes open for interested people:

    In a group Bible study (watch for signs of interest).

    When you are having a conversation on a spiritual topic (Ask, "Would you like to pursue this topic further?").

    When you meet someone that you would like to get to know better (ask him or her out for a meal).

3. Get together for a casual, social time. As you get to know each other during this visit, begin to explore the possibility of establishing a discipling relationship. You can do this by:

    a. Asking a lot of open-ended questions and listening with acceptance.

    b. Asking about the person's walk with God.

    c. Beginning to discern where the person's needs are.

    d. Asking if your friend would like to get together once a week for a few weeks to pursue one of the needs that was mentioned.

4. After you and your friend have decided to meet together on a regular basis with the intent of focusing on the person's growth in Christ, then you can lay more definite plans. The first time you meet "officially," make a personalized survey of your friend's needs and interests. You can do this by asking some of the following questions:

a. When did you first experience a personal relationship with Jesus Christ? How did this come about?

b. What do you appreciate the most about your relationship with Jesus?

c. What were a couple of the most recent high points in this relationship? Why were they so special?

d. Describe what it is like for you to pray.

e. What is it like for you to study the Bible?

f. Have you had any experiences sharing your faith with others? What was that like?

g. In your past experiences, what has helped you grow or change—reading a book? seeing a movie? studying Scripture? playing tennis? going to church?

h. What questions do you have about your faith right now?

i. In what areas of your life would you like to change?

j. How do you think our friendship might help you grow as a Christian?

k. How would you like me to be praying for you as we meet together?

5. With the answers to these questions in mind, you are ready to determine what topic to focus on. It may be an area of spiritual discipline such as prayer, Bible study or quiet time. It may be an area regarding relationships or work, such as marriage, children, parents, time management, self-esteem, dating, decision-making or social justice.

6. Next, determine what materials you will use: books, tapes, movies, articles, interviews, Bible-study guides, conferences or any other materials that seem appropriate.

7. Then think through both of your schedules and determine when and where to meet. Remember to consider:

    a. Where will my friend be most comfortable meeting?

    b. Will we both be free from distractions in this place?

    c. If we are going to focus on prayer, will this place be appropriate?

    d. If we are going to be doing things involving others, do we need to make advance arrangements?

8. Discuss what you will do each time you meet. Allow for at least six to eight meetings together. Make your plans together, giving each other lots of feedback.

9. Finally, be clear about your expectations. Mutually determine:

    a. How do you each expect the other to be involved?

    b. How much preparation time will you each do?

    c. What kind of commitment are you making to each other?

Sample Plan A: Christian Growth   Discipleship Plan Worksheet: How do I grow in my faith?

Week/Date	Purpose	Activity Together	Reflection: Prayer requests? How did it go? What was learned?
1	1. Re-establish relationship. 2. Check out interest level in meeting together. 3. Find out what's happening in Jim's life.	Discuss informally over lunch: what is happening in his life and how God is working in our lives. Suggest meeting regularly to grow as disciples.	Interested in growing. Unclear on specific steps. Eager for direction.
2	1. Focus on Jim's interest in leadership. 2. Get into Scripture. 3. Discover a biblical model for leadership. 4. Share ourselves.	Suggest we read *Excellence in Leadership* by John White (IVP) and a chapter of Nehemiah each week. Share prayer requests and pray.	Has positive response to material. Needs affirmation and encouragement that God is faithful. Pray Jim follows through.
3	1. Be sure there is personal application of key point in book. 2. Encourage, affirm.	Zero in on key point of chapter 1 of book. Discuss application and Jeremiah's style of leadership. Share concerns. Pray. Suggest conference.	How is this person growing? Jim is shy and unwilling to pray together. Really enjoys the book.
4	1. Attend IVCF discipleship training conference: Bible and Life I.	No meeting.	Evaluation of time so far. Any changes needed? Keep going as planned. Gently encourage but don't push prayer together.

Week/Date	Purpose	Activity Together	Reflection: Prayer requests? How did it go? What was learned?
5	1. Share about conference. 2. Discuss Scripture, book. 3. Suggest leadership experience.	Review conference and share key points. Discuss Nehemiah and book chapter. Check out interest/ readiness to attempt specific project.	Good sharing but very general. Unsure what God is teaching Jim. Not ready for special project. Keep praying.
6	1. See movie related to Jim's interests. He is in ROTC and applying to flight school.	See movie Top Gun together.	Learned a lot about Jim's future dreams, interests. He was amazed I wanted to see a movie with him.
7	1. Key in on application of truth. 2. Encourage, affirm. 3. Praise God for answered prayer.	Discuss book, Scripture. Share personal concerns, and pray.	Under lots of pressure—personal demands, struggles with parents. Pray for balance in Jim's life.
8	1. Make plans to continue until we finish book. 2. Ask Jim what has been helpful and what seem to be needs now.	Evaluate our time together, and recommend continuing three more weeks. Praise God for his working.	Evaluation of last seven weeks: Where do we go from here? Recommend we study a scriptural outline of the gospel. Continue to nurture prayer together.

Sample Plan B: Professional, Executive   Discipleship Plan Worksheet

Week/Date	Purpose	Activity Together	Reflection: Prayer requests? How did it go? What was learned?
1	1. Build trust; establish relationship. 2. Share spiritual journey: What has God been doing recently in our lives? 3. Decide when and how often to meet.	Meet for early-morning breakfast together. Get to know each other. Learn areas of interest, issues, concerns, joys, demands. Share prayer requests.	Will meet every other Wednesday. Pray for openness and trust.
2	1. Learn how to support and encourage this person. 2. Agree to share personal monthly calendars with each other to facilitate prayer.	Meet over breakfast. Continue personal sharing. Share prayer requests.	Pray for growing commitment to meet together. Look for ways to help with over-busy schedule.
3	1. Suggest input to our discussion from relevant book.	Catch up on latest business trip. Recommend reading *Ordering Your Private World*. Share prayer requests.	**How is this person growing?** Concern over excellence at work versus excellence in home and church.
4	1. Discuss issue of balance regarding work, relationships, etc. 2. Focus on specific application.	Discuss two chapters of book. Review personal schedule of activities.	**Evaluation of time so far. Any changes needed?** Plan social time together.

Week/Date	Purpose	Activity Together	Reflection: Prayer requests? How did it go? What was learned?
5	1. Informal social time.	Pick him up at the airport from business trip and go out to dinner.	This was a good, fun time—solidified relationship. Need to bring Scripture into discussions.
6	1. Try to make one specific application from book. 2. Share from personal study of Scripture.	Have regular breakfast meeting. Discuss book, upcoming schedule and prayer requests. Describe our quiet time approaches to each other.	Some hesitancy about sharing from Scripture. Good response to book.
7	1. Social time. 2. Share together. 3. Ask about reading same passage of Scripture.	Attend concert together. Have snack afterward. Agree to read same passage to discuss: Ecclesiastes 3:1-14.	**How is this person growing?** We are making slow progress. Studying Ecclesiastes passage will relate well to work issues.
8	1. Continue book discussion. 2. Work to apply one truth from Ecclesiastes 3. 3. Pray together.	Have breakfast meeting. Discuss book and Ecclesiastes. Pray.	**Evaluation of last seven weeks: Where do we go from here?** Suggest we continue meeting to finish book and share together over at least two more passages.

Discipleship Plan Worksheet

Week/Date	Purpose	Activity Together	Reflection: Prayer requests? How did it go? What was learned?
1			
2			
3			
4			Evaluation of time so far: Any changes needed?

Week/Date	Purpose	Activity Together	Reflection: Prayer requests? How did it go? What was learned?
5			
6			
7			
8			Evaluation of last seven weeks: Where do we go from here?

9
HOW TO MODEL THE CHRISTIAN LIFE

The small fried-chicken restaurant near where I live advertises that "the Colonel does it better." If there is ever a time when I am convinced that this is true, it is when I walk by the restaurant on an empty stomach. The aroma of fried chicken engulfs me. My stomach juices start to flow. My mouth waters. Even if I hadn't noticed hunger before, I suddenly feel starved. The smell of food cooking does more than all the advertising in the world to convince me that I want to buy that chicken.

The Bible says that we are to smell like Christ. We are to God the "aroma of Christ among those who are being saved and those who are perishing" (2 Cor 2:15). We are "incense offered by Christ to God" (NEB). We are the fragrance of Christ to the world. We are to make people hungry for Jesus. We are to make them salivate spiritually.

An aroma is not visible. You cannot touch it. It is hard to define. But it is very much present, more so perhaps than what we can see and touch. As disciplemakers, the aroma of our lives should so permeate the atmosphere that those we meet will want to meet Jesus.

This happened to me as a child when I met Mrs. Delaney. The Delaneys lived about four houses away. The Delaney children were older than I was, so I didn't see them often. But their house, and Mrs. Delaney in particular, smelled of Christ! I never remember her "preaching" to me, but years later, when I wanted to grow as a Christian, I thought to myself, "I want to be like Mrs. Delaney."

Soon afterward, I decided I wanted to be like my sister. Her new-found faith was important to her, so I decided my faith should be important to me. She read her Bible every day, so I read my Bible daily. She got involved in a fellowship group on her campus, so I joined a Christian group in my high school. She went to church, so I went to church.

Then I decided I wanted to be like Mrs. Delaney's daughter, Karen. Karen was a happy person, so I tried to smile more. Karen was gracious, so I tried to be more friendly. Karen was also popular. So, with a bit of self-centered motivation, I thought that if I copied Karen, I would be popular. This reflects the kind of precision Paul describes in Philippians 1:15-18—the right actions for the wrong reasons. Nevertheless, God is sovereign.

A Reason for Imitation

As much as we all long to be unique individuals, we spend much of our lives imitating others. And this is not all bad. Michael Griffiths in *The Example of Jesus* writes that "imitating others is a mark of being human. In all human societies people watch other people—and this has been the way in which civilization has made progress. One man discovers the wheel and others imitate him, and find further uses for it. Someone else discovers that strawberries are good to eat, and others follow his example in collecting and eating wild strawberries. . . . Everyone is forever watching everyone else."[1]

Our job as disciplemakers is to provide models that are worthy of imitation. This is a biblical concept. Paul wrote to the Christians in Thessalonica, "You became imitators of us and of the Lord. . . . And so you became a model to all the believers in Macedonia and Achaia" (1 Thess 1:6-7). The Hebrew Christians of the New Testament church were told, "Remember your leaders, who spoke the word of God to you. Consider the outcome of their way of life and imitate their faith" (Heb 13:7). "We do not want you to become lazy, but to imitate those who through faith and patience inherit what has been promised" (Heb 6:12). Imitation is a way of learning, a way of growing.

Paul was very aware of this in his own ministry. He went so far as to say to the Corinthians, "I urge you to imitate me" (1 Cor 4:16). He wrote to Timothy, "What you have heard from me, keep as the pattern of sound teaching" (2 Tim 1:13). Does that sound audacious? It does to me! Personally, I think Paul had a lot of nerve. But as we will see, it was that nerve which enabled him to be an effective discipler of young Christians.

I am not suggesting that we run around telling people to imitate us. Rather, we should humbly remember the powerful influence of the example of our lives. In his classic work, *Rhetoric,* Aristotle wrote, a few hundred years before Jesus lived, that the character of the speaker "may almost be called the most effective means of persuasion he possessed." When God became a man, his influence among us was greater than any words or arguments.

Imitation is a fact of life. It happens all the time. John warned his friend Gaius, "Do not imitate what is evil but what is good" (3 Jn 11). If people do not imitate what is good, they will imitate what is evil. Think of what happens at a social gathering when one person tells a story with a slight exaggeration here and there. Soon the next person jumps in, telling another story with more exaggeration. Before long a whole group of people are telling stories, and truth and falsehood become indistinguishable.

But our example can influence others for good. Several Sundays ago, as I hustled through last-minute details before church, I noticed that my pastor is always in his seat about ten minutes before the service starts. I thought to myself, "I want to do that. Next Sunday I'll come a little earlier." I wanted to imitate what I saw in my pastor. Now I have him to thank when I am more prepared to worship on Sunday mornings.

Part of being the salt of the earth, or being light in a fallen world, is being an example of God's good work to men and women today. Part of disciplemaking is modeling.

What do you think of when you think of a model? For some, the image that comes to mind is that of a mannequin in a store window. This is not the Christian meaning of modeling. The mannequin in the window looks lovely—unless you happen to walk by when the window is being "dressed." When that happens, you may see a headless figure, or one with its arm removed and being stuffed into a sleeve. At best, you will see on the undressed mannequin all the artificial joints and fixtures which are designed to make it look so good on the outside.

This is not the kind of model we are to be. We will not be perfect, and we must never be fake. As we become disciplemakers, we must be willing to let people see the inside, so that they will know that true beauty, which is worth imitating, comes from Jesus and not from artificial props.

Paul may have sounded audacious to some, but he was also able to admit his faults. "Even though I was once a blasphemer and a persecutor and a violent man, I was shown mercy" (1 Tim 1:13). He wrote publicly that he was "less than the least of all God's people" (Eph 3:8). He was not afraid to let people see his weaknesses because those weaknesses showed God's strengths. It was probably this freedom to be real which enabled Paul to say to the Thessalonians, "We loved you so much that we were delighted to share with you not only the gospel of God but our lives as well" (1 Thess 2:8).

This should be our perspective in disciplemaking—to share our lives with our friends in such a way that they will be drawn to love Jesus as Lord. As we share ourselves with young Christians, we are not inviting them to move into our lives, lock, stock and barrel. Rather, we are inviting them to look into the windows of our hearts.

When young Christians look into the hearts of their disciplemakers, what will they see? It is hoped, they will see a love for Jesus, a confidence in the Bible, a commitment to prayer, a desire to learn and grow, and a love for other people. These characteristics are at the heart of the disciplemaking process. Let's look at each of these qualities as though we were looking into the windows of disciplemakers' lives and see what there is to imitate.

A Love for Jesus

When young Christians look at the lives of older Christians, they will be drawn to imitate them if they see that the persons are comfortable with the Lord. There are those individuals who seem to so love the Lord that each day is a genuine response of obedience to him. Their faith is not a religion tacked on to their lives but a relationship with Jesus which permeates every decision they make. One of the things that immediately draws me to want to imitate other persons is when I see them sincerely integrating their faith into their everyday experiences. When they let me see that they love Jesus in spite of daily struggles, and that they must struggle themselves in order to love Jesus more, then I say to myself, "I can relate to them. They have problems in their lives, but they seem to handle them with faith. Maybe I can learn something from the way they do that." It is not problem-free people whom we long to imitate but people who live life in light of their love for Jesus.

A Confidence in the Bible

Disciplemakers will also want to model a confidence in the Bible as God's Word. Part of disciplemaking is sharing with your young Christian friend how God has taught you and helped you through the influence of Scripture. The Word of God needs to have cut through your own life before you can convince your friend that his Word is "sharper than any double-edged sword" (Heb 4:12).

A friend of mine had an interesting experience while visiting with an older Christian couple. My friend, Heidi, needed to borrow a Bible while she was staying in the Fryes' home. Using Carolyn Frye's Bible was a moving experience for Heidi. In the margins she saw frequent references to dates when particular passages had been helpful. She also saw names beside certain promises of Scripture, and she remembered that Carolyn was apt to say, "I prayed today that God would help you in such-and-such a way." Heidi could see that Carolyn took the Word of God seriously and that she prayed expectantly, in light of what God promised he would do.

Few people have the opportunity to see into another's spiritual life as Heidi did. And many of us might be shy about sharing our intimate prayers as Carolyn did in lending her Bible. But if we are going to make disciples, the margins of our daily lives should be filled with evidence, both verbal and nonverbal, that we live the truths of Scripture.

A Commitment to Prayer

Disciplemakers must be examples of ones who pray. What touched Heidi so much when she read Carolyn's Bible was not just that Carolyn read Scripture, but that she *prayed*. Carolyn used to say to Heidi that if someone's name popped into her mind during the day, she took that as a reminder from God to pray for that person. Often she would follow up her prayer with a note or a phone call.

One of my own goals in life is to undertake only those projects or relationships that I do have time to pray about. As I disciple young Christians, I share with them my struggles to meet this goal and the joy it is to see God answer prayer.

A Desire to Learn and Grow

Living on the growing edge of life may be one of the most important parts of our example to young Christians. This means being creative and biblical in problem solving, being open to new ideas, being curious and being willing to change. If we model this, we give our younger Christian friends a good model to imitate.

The people I admire are not cemented to their thought patterns. They know what they believe, and they love Jesus with conviction, but they realize that growth means change. They are open to God healing their blind spots and giving them new wisdom in old areas of truth.

The challenge to change becomes most acute in the areas that are most important to us. I saw Andrea struggle in this way. Andrea is a beautiful woman. Her clothes are stylish, her physique enviable, her manner sophisticated. And her appearance is important to her. Sometimes too important. So when Andrea met Sylvia, she was not overly impressed. Sylvia is plain, not someone you would notice walking down the street. But as Andrea got to know Sylvia, she was drawn to her, not by her outward appearance, but by her love for Jesus and her genuine concern for others. This had the effect of challenging the value Andrea placed on outward appearance. She decided that she would place more emphasis on growing her spiritual, inward life and less emphasis on outward beauty. Andrea struggled with this, but she decided to make changes and to live on the growing edge of her life.

But the story does not end here. Andrea told her friend Susan about Sylvia. Susan doesn't worry much about appearances, but she does have strong opinions about life. After learning about Andrea's willingness to change, Susan said to herself, "Maybe I should be more willing to make some changes in my life." And so the aroma of Jesus spread.

A Love for Other People

One of my friends is Jeanie, a student at the university near where I live. I asked Jeanie who had influenced her the most to grow as a Christian. She immediately thought of an older Christian woman who had let her look into the windows of her life. Jeanie liked what she saw. She liked the way her friend, Lois, related to her peers at work. She liked the way Lois reached out to people at church. She liked what she saw as Lois worked out her faith on a day-by-day basis. And Jeanie liked the way Lois reached out to her.

As Lois shared her life with Jeanie, Jeanie said she grew in the confidence that she too could be a Christian leader. Lois talked to her on a mature level. She shared herself with Jeanie, taking Jeanie beyond her own current experience. Jeanie felt loved because Lois cared about who Jeanie could become. Jeanie watched Lois. Lois loved Jeanie. And Jeanie grew.

Young Christians look into the lives of their disciplemakers, they need to see a genuine, active love for others. The opposite of love is self-absorption. We need to be very aware of the influence we have on others, but we dare not let that awareness become preoccupation with ourselves. We become good models, people who are worthy to imitate, in the privacy of our own relationships with Jesus. Then when we go out into the world, we forget who we are. We need to lose self-consciousness as we reach out to help meet the needs of others, to care for them as a reflection of God's care for us.

Notes
[1]Michael Griffiths, *The Example of Jesus* (Downers Grove, Ill.: InterVarsity Press, 1985), p. 13.

Putting It All Together
1. As you remember the powerful influence of the example of your life, how does it make you feel?

2. Take some time to reflect on what you may be modeling to others. Meditate on the following questions, asking God to show you how you can become a more mature model of a follower of Jesus.

On the love of Christ: If Jesus were suddenly no longer a part of your life, what difference would it make?

What feelings do you have for Jesus?

How do you express them?

On Scripture: How do you talk about what you are learning from Scripture?

How deep is your conviction that Scripture is true even when God seems silent or distant?

On prayer: Whom are you praying for?

How recently have you experienced answers to prayer, and what were they?

On the desire to grow: In what way have you been changing in some area of your life?

How often do you expose yourself to new ideas?

On love for others: When was the last time you sacrificed in your personal life for another person (giving emotional or physical energy, time, money, etc.)?

How much has it cost you to love that person?

3. Paul wrote to Timothy: "You . . . know all about my teaching, my way of life, my purpose, faith, patience, love, endurance,

persecutions, sufferings" (2 Tim 3:10). What friends know that much about you?

Think of one person who will be very honest with you. Ask him or her what influence you have had on his or her life.

Resource on Modeling the Christian Life

Am I Ready to Be a Disciplemaker?

It is often easier to sense the aroma of Christ in someone else's life than in our own. This means that many Christians need reassurance that they are modeling a life worth imitating. Survey your own life with the following questions.

1. List three questions you have right now about yourself, God, your life or life in general.

2. What is something you learned about God last week?

3. What is something you learned recently from Scripture?

4. How often have you had a quiet time (or personal devotions) in the last month?

5. What was your involvement in your local church last month?

6. List ten things you really enjoy doing.

How has God used any of these activities to give you relationships with other people that help them grow in their faith?

7. List three things you identify as strengths in your life.

8. What are three weaknesses in your life that you would like to see change?

9. What are you doing this year to serve your church or Christian group?

10. Whom do you know who is a Christian and needs encouragement to grow?

11. Whom do you know who is not a Christian but might be interested in becoming one?

12. What people have influenced you the most to grow as a Christian, and how did they influence you?

13. Look at question six. Whom do you know who also enjoys doing some of these things? How can you encourage this person to grow spiritually?

14. What three things are the biggest barriers in your life to becoming a disciplemaker?

What would help you overcome each barrier?

15. Look over the answers you have written here. Do you think you are ready to be a disciplemaker?

If not, what changes do you think you need to make before you are ready?

If you are ready to be a disciplemaker, ask God to lead you to someone to disciple. Begin praying for three people, expecting that at least one will be interested in meeting with you.

Book Study: The Fight

John White's book *The Fight* gives helpful instruction on how to grow as a Christian. The following book study is designed to be used by a disciplemaker and a friend. See if you can find someone to study this book with you.

Sample Book Study Schedule

Book   _The Fight,_ John White

Date _____

Unit	Personal Preparation	Activities to Do Together
1	Read chapter 1.	Read Mt 28:16-20. What is Jesus' vision for the world? How does he want to accomplish it? Pray that you will have a vision for your world.
2	Read chapters 2 and 3.	Read Jn 4:1-30. How did Jesus build trust? Think of a non-Christian friend. How can you build trust with that person? Pray for that friend.
3	No reading.	Exercise: Find someone sitting alone on campus, and start a conversation about anything. Debrief over ice cream afterward.
4	Read chapters 4 and 5.	Study Jn 8:1-11. Describe Jesus' compassion and actions. How do you relate to the sins of those around you? Pray for non-Christian friends.
5	Review "First Steps to God" (see p. 175).	Exercise: Role-play telling the gospel to each other. Mark areas on which you need to work. Go to a movie with a non-Christian friend.
6	Read chapters 6 and 7.	Have a meal together. Talk about your changing feelings and observations about evangelism. Pray together.
7	Read chapter 8.	Exercise: Start a conversation with someone this week, and ask, "Are you interested in spiritual things?" Debrief afterward. Pray together.
8	Read chapters 9 and 10.	Study Lk 10:25-37. What are the characteristics of a good "neighbor"? How does this relate to evangelism? Pray together.
9	Read chapters 11 and 12.	Visit the student union or another campus gathering spot. Ask several students if they would like to talk about spiritual issues. Debrief.
10	No reading.	Study Acts 17:16-34. What is the heart of the gospel? Write down three intentions you have as a result of these ten weeks together. Pray together.

10
HOW TO HELP PEOPLE WHO HURT

Deborah was sobbing. Through her tears she told me about the time she had been sexually abused as a young child. When she told her mother about the incident, her mother responded, "That's dirty! Go take a bath." They never talked about it again.

As a result, Deborah decided that she would never, ever again discuss anything of consequence with her mother. When I met her, the wounds from this trauma still remained deep within her. Not only did she have difficulty trusting her mother, it also became difficult for her to trust *anyone*, especially men. She disliked herself intensely, though she was a delightful person and had much to offer. For me to ask her to trust God and to experience his love was an overwhelming request. As trust was established between us in a discipling relationship, these serious problems continued to come out.

Deborah's situation was tragic, but it is not unique. As we disciple others, we can expect to be touching wounded people. The love and acceptance of a discipling relationship often provides a safe place where deep wounds can be uncovered. Some of these wounds may have been hidden for years. Some may be much more current.

There is my friend who just had an abortion and is now being eaten up by the guilt. Or the young woman from my church who was raised in a Christian home, became pregnant out of wedlock and now is being totally rejected by her family. Many around me are hurting because of divorce in their families or because they have been divorced themselves. Drugs and alcohol are tragically common.

Sin may be no more common today than in the past, but I sense that people are feeling more isolated in dealing with their sin, disappointments, frustrations and failures. Our world is becoming increasingly complex and mechanized. Churches are becoming bigger and busier. People are becoming lonelier and lonelier. If there has ever been a time when people need support and understanding and forgiveness, it is now.

It used to be that discipling and counseling were thought of as two totally separate entities. It is no longer possible to make this separation. We do not need to be professional counselors in order to be disciplemakers, but we need to remember that as we seek to make disciples and to influence friends for the sake of the kingdom, we will often find ourselves relating to people who hurt. More often that not, the individuals we want to disciple will have wounds and scars from past battles. We may find ourselves asking what to do when these wounds erupt before our eyes.

As Deborah sobbed, I felt helpless. I prayed quietly for wisdom. I listened intently as she talked. I sat close to her and put my hand on hers. I asked questions that would help her to say what she wanted to say. She felt intense anger at being abused by someone who should have been taking care of her. And yet she also felt that she was somehow responsible for the incident. Years of hatred and anger had been suppressed, causing headaches, abdominal pain and bitterness. She was afraid of her own anger. It needed to be reached and expressed. There were episodes of explosions and verbal outbursts. I had to learn not to take these personally. She needed to ventilate this anger without judgment and guilt. Only then could she move on toward health.

When someone opens up to us in such a way, our initial response is very important. As Deborah told me later, if I had shown shock or expressed disbelief, she would never have said anything more about it to me. Shock, withdrawal, judgment or another negative response would have slammed the door shut for her—again.

As she talked, I was indeed shocked—but not at Deborah. I was shocked by sin and saddened by evil. Sometimes, as in Deborah's situation, the devastating effect of sin is imposed on another. But at other times we will find ourselves discipling young Christians who are suffering from the results of their own sinful choices. In either case, we need to be careful to provide a haven where the battle with sin can be won.

Havens of Rest

God understands that his people need places of restoration. He led the Israelites to Elim, an oasis in the desert (Ex 15:27). Elijah was touched by God as he slept under a broom tree (1 Kings 19). David praised God for green pastures and quiet waters (Ps 23). Our job as disciplemakers will sometimes take the form of inviting people to a place of emotional healing and restoration.

What does this place look like? How can we extend the invitation to come? How can we be God's agents in ministering to hurting people?

Let us remember, first of all, that this haven, this oasis, is God's place, not ours. We are inviting our friends to meet the living God who heals and gives health. We will not have all the answers. We will not fix the problems. We will not bring about healing.

There are many extreme views about how God redeems through healing. My convictions about it are simple: God is sovereign. God heals. He desires healing for us. There is a spiritual battle raging. Sometimes there are casualties. We do not always see God's victory in its completeness this side of heaven. In fact, we will not be truly whole until we see Jesus face to face. Sometimes God allows suffering to teach us obedience (Heb 5:8). Sometimes he allows pain in one part of our lives in order to bring healing in another part. Sometimes we may never have a satisfying explanation for our pain.

So I cannot promise health, wealth and happiness to the one I disciple. But I can promise that God is at work, healing and refining, and that someday the process will be complete.

So then, as we disciple others, we invite them to a place where God heals and redeems. We invite them to discover his love. We invite them to a place of peace.

It is God's place. It is his invitation. We are his hosts and hostesses. I would like to suggest three things we as his ministers can do to facilitate healing: listen, reflect and give feedback.

Listen

First we need to help our hurting friends come to terms with the problem at hand. I like the way Proverbs 20:5 says it: "The purposes of a man's heart are deep waters, but a man of understanding draws them out."

We are all equipped with two instruments which are most effective in drawing out a friend. They are called ears.

With our ears, we listen, listen, listen as our friends tell us about the wounds in their lives which need healing. Sometimes friends seem distant and only want to talk a little. Then we listen a little. Sometimes friends seem to want to talk but don't know how to begin. Then we ask questions which implicitly communicate that we are willing to listen to whatever is said. And sometimes friends are open and anxious to talk. Then we listen with eagerness. Listening, in itself, is one of the things God uses to heal his people.

In this context, let me tell you about one of the mysteries of my own life. While a student and later after I had graduated, I began to see people being healed before my eyes. Time and again I would talk with people who were in emotional pain. Many times they left the conversations with more peace, less pain and more hope. And I did not know why. In the course of these conversations, I did nothing to change the circumstances of their lives. Sometimes we talked about Scripture. Sometimes we did not. I always tried to come with an attitude of prayer, depending on the Holy Spirit's work, but seldom did we bow our heads, fold our hands and pray. So where did this healing come from? I couldn't figure it out.

But now I think I know. I found out through an insight from Ken Blue in his book *Authority to Heal*. He wrote:

Intense listening is indistinguishable from love, and love heals. This kind of listening means that the people receiving attention are allowed to be the experts on their own pain. . . . This kind of listening not only builds up and heals, it also encourages people in need toward deeper self-disclosure through increased trust.[1]

This insight helped me to see that God, the Holy Spirit, had been using my ears as his instruments of healing. What a privilege that was for me. Since then, I have learned to value listening even more, both as a listener and as one who has received from others the gift of being heard.

Never forget that you will be of more help when you use your ears than when you use your mouth. Sometimes we tire of listening before our friends tire of talking. When that happens, we need to shore up and keep listening.

People almost always learn more from what they say than from what they hear. This is especially true for the person in pain. Very often, it is difficult for hurting people to talk about the source of their pain. Adult children of alcoholics find it difficult to admit that their parents drank. It was hard for Deborah to talk about incest. And it is almost always hard to talk about pain which we have inflicted on ourselves. As you disciple hurting people, you will undoubtedly hear, "Oh, I can't talk about it." But only as your friend does talk about "it," does "it" become something which can indeed be faced and healed.

We can draw out people in pain by loving responses such as, "I want to listen, if you want to tell me more," or "How did that make you feel?" Sometimes a touch, a hug or praying together communicate that we care and are willing to hurt with the pain that hurts our friends.

One of the greatest barriers to listening is our propensity to think that we have to offer answers. It is easy to fall into the subtle temptation of thinking that we are responsible for the healing of others' wounds. This assumption has dire consequences. If we don't have advice to give, we may feel so helpless that we withdraw, leaving our friends alone once again.

Actually, rather than being overly responsible or withdrawing, we need to recognize that it is not primarily answers which our friends need. Henri Nouwen in *Out of Solitude* observes:

The basic meaning of care is: to grieve, to experience sorrow, to cry out with. . . . We feel quite uncomfortable with an invitation to enter into someone's pain before doing something about it. Still, when we honestly ask ourselves which persons in our lives mean the most to us, we often find that it is those who, instead of giving much advice, solutions, or cures, have chosen rather to share our pain and touch our wounds with a gentle and tender hand.[2]

Most of the time this is all we can do. We cannot solve the problems. We *can* offer hope. We can stand firm in that hope when our friends are too weak to hold their own. We can offer the confidence that this fallen world will not self-destruct. God is actively involved in our lives. He wants to redeem. He wants to love us.

Reflect and Clarify

As we draw out our friends' pain by listening, we can also help by reflecting back what we hear. This helps the individuals clarify the problems as well as their own positions in relationship to the problems. We can facilitate this clarification with comments like,

"What I hear you saying is . . ."

"When that happened, did you feel like . . . ?"

"Are you saying that . . . ?"

All of these questions will help draw out the thoughts, feelings and pain our friends are experiencing. They will understand themselves better as they respond, and increased self-awareness is always part of growth and healing.

Give Feedback

But the process of helping a friend in pain does not end with listening and reflecting. At some point, we also need to give feedback. Do not be misled by the image of the patient on the couch and the passive doctor taking notes. As God's ministers, we are equipped to help, to speak his words.

Just remember that the feedback you give is a very small part of the healing process. If we are not misled by the fear that we have nothing to offer, we may be misled by offering too much. If you are doing more than forty per cent of the talking, consider closing your mouth and opening your ears.

As you listen, prayerfully consider the situation your friend is describing. Then you can begin giving feedback in three areas: believing and praying, applying Scripture and discussing forgiveness.

Believing and Praying. You may want to ask your friend, "Would you let me believe for you that God will work in your life until you can believe for yourself?"

Just the other day I had lunch with a friend who was experiencing deep pain. I listened to her complaints and her fears. She was not ready to hope. So I reminded her of the four men who cut a hole through the roof to lower their paralyzed friend down to Jesus. I said to my friend, "Would you let me carry you to Jesus in prayer? I believe he will heal you, even though you may not believe that yet." She was willing to let me pray.

Applying Scripture. We may want to share with our friends situations in Scripture that are similar to the ones they are experiencing. The Bible is full of the pathos of human need. Perhaps what helped people in Scripture will help our friends also. David suffered from his adultery. Abraham suffered from his own lies. Sarah had a hard time believing God. Leah and Rachel were in a love triangle. How did God work things out for these people? Did he say anything to them which would be helpful to our friends? Does Scripture speak to the problems they are dealing with? Very gently, you may come along beside your friend and look together for answers in Scripture.

Discussing Forgiveness. And, finally, when we reach out to friends in pain, we almost always need to spend time talking about forgiveness. Any discussion of forgiveness needs to be on two levels: Our need to receive forgiveness, both from God and from others; and our need to forgive those who have sinned against us.

Forgiveness was an important issue for Deborah. We talked many times after she first told me about her past. We talked about her relationship with her mother. We talked about what it would be like for her to forgive her mother. We talked about forgiving others in her life also. We talked about how forgiveness is a process and how it may take time and many, many forgivings until the heart is clear. Deborah and I talked about the fact that we cannot be healed if we do not forgive, that without forgiveness we continue to destroy ourselves. And we talked about what it means that God has forgiven us.

Receiving Forgiveness

When people are in the process of being healed, they almost always begin to see how their own sin has contributed to their pain. Deborah was an innocent victim of sin, yet even she needed to come to grips with her own sinfulness apart from the situation of her abuse. When the healing process involves the admission of personal sin, we can provide the environment where our friend can respond to the conviction of the Holy Spirit. We can reflect to our friends the God who is not shocked or surprised by their sin. Isaiah tells us that Jesus is gentle: "A bruised reed he will not break, and a smoldering wick he will not snuff out" (Is 42:3). In our loving responses to our friends' confessions, we can imitate Jesus.

Then we can remind them of the good news that God will forgive. When we are disciplers, we are also priests. Not that we dole out expiation and forgiveness, but as priests we bring our friends to God to receive his forgiveness. Sometimes this takes the form of reminding them that they need to forgive themselves for what God has already forgiven them. Sometimes it will mean that we need to pray out loud together, acknowledging God's forgiveness. Then, based on God's Word, we can pronounce our friends forgiven (Jn 20:22-23).

Let me add a word of caution, however. Receiving forgiveness is often a process. Do not be too quick to reassure people of God's forgiveness. They may leave your encounter full of intentions to reform and to continue to experience God's graciousness. But because God gives people freedom, they may turn around and choose to sin again. If you see them continuing to make wrong choices, it may be that they have not really understood God's perspective on their lives. In that case, you probably need to do a Bible study together on the issue at hand or read a book or listen to a tape on the topic. Perhaps another person, such as a pastor or a Christian counselor, needs to be brought into the relationship.

On the other hand, there are those who may be aware of God's will on the issue and do not care to change. Such situations have been very hard on me. I see the destruction and pain, but I cannot force change. I can pray faithfully; I can continue to love and be a friend. But ultimately the decision to change belongs to my friends. I have to live with that, even as they have to live with the consequences of their decisions.

Extending Forgiveness

As you disciple others, you will also need to help them learn to forgive those who have sinned against them. Often we will find that those we are discipling need to extend forgiveness before they can really appreciate the fact that God has forgiven them. It may be that they have been deeply hurt, as Deborah was. Or perhaps it is a matter of small hurts which have built up a wall of resentment over the years. We may be able to help young disciples extend forgiveness by talking about the pervasiveness of sin.

Sometimes forgiveness comes when we realize that "there but for the grace of God go I." Or sometimes it comes when we remember that those who offended us may be so emotionally damaged themselves that it is as if they were paralyzed emotionally. So we extend to them the same understanding we would to ones who are paralyzed physically. Sometimes extending forgiveness comes very, very slowly. But it is always part of the healing process.

Notice that when we are helping friends who hurt, we are offering to listen, to reflect and to give feedback, but we are not "rescuing" them. We rescue people who are drowning by holding them up above water, swimming for them if they are too weak, even breathing for them if they need artificial respiration. But this is not the way to help people in pain. We must not solve their problems for them, take over the affairs of their lives or assume inappropriate responsibility for their needs. That would create an artificial support system that would not give lasting strength and help.

Instead of giving temporary help, let us invite our friends to the place of eternal healing. Let us draw them out, listening and responding with gentleness. Let us invite them to hope, to believe the God of Scripture, to forgive and to be forgiven. In this environment, healing often occurs. This rarely happens quickly. And sometimes the process seems incomplete. But God is at work; he will accomplish his purposes.

Often as I disciple friends who are in pain and we wait together to see God at work, I share with them my own struggles. Sometimes, however, my own experience is so different from theirs that I need to go to the library or talk to other people to find out all I can about their situations. Sometimes I suggest they get professional counseling or go to a support group for people with similar needs. Sometimes I try to help by being supportive in other ways—with sending a note, making a call, cleaning a house when a friend is too depressed to function, taking in a meal, going to church with someone, sharing a meal out or offering a special book with words of appreciation and encouragement.

In all of this, perhaps my highest responsibility is to pray. "The prayer of a righteous [person] is powerful and effective" (Jas

5:16). When people are praying for me, I know that they love me. I try to give this love gift to others.

My relationship with Deborah has continued over many years. Quite a few other painful wounds have been opened up. There have been times when I have desired healing and change in her life much more quickly than they have occurred. There have been growth spurts that have been refreshing and wonderful. But Deborah still has difficulty forgiving her parents, and she is continuing to suffer because of this. Even so, God is at work in her and loves her more than I ever could. Someday Jesus will meet Deborah in heaven and "he will wipe every tear from [her] eyes" (Rev 21:4). In the meantime it is a special privilege for me to be an agent of his love for her on earth.

Notes
[1]Ken Blue, *Authority to Heal* (Downers Grove, Ill.: InterVarsity Press, 1987), p. 128.
[2]Henri Nouwen, *Out of Solitude* (Notre Dame, Ind.: Ave Maria Press, 1974), p. 34.

Putting It All Together
1. Describe a situation where you experienced God's comfort through a friend.
How did your friend make the initial offer to help?
How did you feel about your friend's care for you?
Which of your friend's actions helped you the most?
How did this experience prepare you to help someone else who is suffering?
2. Why is listening more important than talking when helping a friend who hurts?
3. Which of the following phrases do you use most often in responding to a friend in need?
"You should . . ."

"You need to . . ."
"I'm sorry you feel . . ."
"I wish . . ."
What do you think is helpful or non-helpful in each phrase?
4. Describe the posture of those who listen in a helpful way. How do they sit? What do they do with their hands? their eyes? their feet? What difference does posture make?
5. List five characteristics you know about God which comfort you when you are hurting.
How would you go about communicating this good news to a friend?
6. How do you think you would have responded to Deborah?
What did the author do which was different from what you might do?
If you were Deborah, how would you want people to respond to you?
7. Look up 2 Corinthians 1:3-5. Rewrite the verses in your own words, substituting your name for the personal pronouns and adding the name of a friend after "those in any trouble."
Pray for the opportunity to pass on God's comfort.

Resource on Helping People Who Hurt

When and How to Get Professional Counseling Help
1. The question is often asked, "How do I know when I need (or my friend needs) professional help?" The following symptoms may indicate that you are dealing with problems too difficult to handle alone:
☐ The problem persists for many months, with no resolution in sight.
☐ You feel as if you "have all the answers" but don't know how to apply them to your situation.
☐ You feel very depressed for several weeks at a time for no

apparent reason.

☐ Thoughts of suicide or other abnormal behavior intrude frequently into your thinking.

2. If professional counseling is necessary, the following suggestions will help you find a counselor:

☐ The relationship between the counselor and client is very unique and very intimate. Look for someone you feel comfortable with. If the first counselor doesn't work out, look for another.

☐ Ask a friend, a pastor, a doctor or someone else you respect for a recommendation for a good counselor. Board certification is one thing to look for, but personal recommendation is probably even more important. If you have no one to ask, looking in the yellow pages of the phone book is better than not going at all.

☐ Try to speak with the counselor by phone before the first appointment. Even a phone conversation will give you an idea of whether or not you will be able to relate to the counselor. Ask about his or her professional certification, and ask what approach the counselor uses. Ask about the person's professional background (this should tell you how much experience the person has had in counseling). Ask too how the counselor's spiritual values influence his or her counseling.

☐ It is good if your counselor is a believer, but don't assume that a non-Christian counselor cannot be helpful. Likewise, don't assume that just because someone is a Christian that he or she will be a good counselor.

☐ Once you begin to see the counselor, ask for an assessment of your situation and the counselor's tentative goals for your counseling experience. The counselor won't be able to hand you "all the answers" but should be insightful and goal oriented.

☐ When you go for counseling, be as open, as honest and as specific as you can be about your own needs and feelings. Your participation in your counseling experience is even more important than your counselor's in terms of the success of your therapy

11
HOW PEOPLE CHANGE

Jesus' ministry had the effect of changing people. In fact, if people did not change their behavior, he indicated that they had not really heard him at all. On one occasion, he said to the people listening, "Why do you call me, 'Lord, Lord,' and do not do what I say?" (Lk 6:46). In Matthew's account, he was even more blunt: "Not everyone who says to me, 'Lord, Lord,' will enter the kingdom of heaven, but only he who does the will of my Father who is in heaven" (Mt 7:21).

If we want to be disciplemakers, we too will be asking people to make changes. This is one of the most difficult aspects of disciplemaking. We may be able to find someone to disciple. We may build a loving relationship with that person. And we may have wonderful ideas about how to disciple the individual. But all of this is useless if our friend does not mature in Christ, making the change from a life centering around self to a life centering around the Lord Jesus Christ.

Change is not primarily an intellectual choice, although the intellect is involved. The kinds of changes we are talking about are rooted in our internal desires. We all know that lifestyle changes will be temporary at best unless we really want to make them. This is why I did not start a regular exercise program for years even after I learned that exercise is important to my health. I intellectually endorsed something that I was not willing to personally embrace.

And this is why my friend Beth did not change when I tried to convince her that a life based on biblical principles would be better for her than her self-centered existence. For two years I shared my life with her, suggesting changes that would benefit her, and trying in every way I could to nurture her into discipleship. But nothing worked. Then she went to the Urbana Missionary Conference. What an experience! She came back and told me all she had discovered. I had to swallow my pride when I realized that changes were accomplished in five days which I had tried to initiate for years. Somehow at Urbana, Beth was ready to internalize her need for change, to make it her own choice.

Our resistance to change is not all bad. It provides a built-in mechanism for making sure that the change is good. If we changed with every suggestion, we would be chameleons, not human beings. So when we question change, we may be asking, "Does this change make sense? How will it affect me? Will its effect be good?"

But those of us who want to be disciplemakers are already convinced that the change from self-sufficiency to commitment to Jesus is good. In fact, it is the best change any person can ever make. The problem is, how do we convince our friends? What can we do to help our friends want to become disciples? What can we do to help our friends change?

The first thing we can do to help friends want to change is to model in our lives attitudes and values that prompt them to want to change their own. Madeleine L'Engle wrote in *Walking on Water*:

> We do not draw people to Christ by loudly discrediting what they believe, by telling them how wrong they are and how right we are, but by showing them a light that is so lovely that they want with all their hearts to know the source of it.[1]

If our lives are peaceful, truthful and joyful, then those who rub shoulders with us will notice, and some who are not yet active disciples may become ready to change.

The impetus to change comes in many forms. It comes as hope. It comes as involvement. And it comes as information. As disciplemakers we cannot cause people to change. But we can provide a climate where hope, involvement and information can work their best to effect motivation for change.

Hope
Milton Mayeroff wrote about hope when he observed:

> In caring for another person, I inspire him to have the courage to be himself. My trust in him encourages him to trust himself and to be worthy of the trust. Perhaps few things are more encouraging to another than to realize that his growth evokes admiration, a spontaneous delight or joy, in the one who cares for him.[2]

I have a friend who cares for me and hopes in me like that. His care is not the oppressive embrace of someone trying to mold me into what he wants me to be. It is the invigorating support of someone who believes in my abilities and rejoices in my successes. He tells me what he enjoys about me. He tells me why he respects me. He expresses love for me even when I fail miserably. When he gives me suggestions, I sense that he is on my side, working with me as I change—not trying to change me by his help.

Scripture gives us a framework for hope. We see again and again that God looks at us not as we are now, but as we will be. I am intrigued by the reference in Revelation 2:17 to the new name Jesus will give me in heaven. That name is a secret now, but I suspect it will reflect the person he is hoping I will become, by his grace. I also suspect that he calls me by my new name now, even though I am still becoming. I do know that Jesus has enough hope, not just in me, but in his work in my life, to promise to stand beside me and present me "without fault" to his Father (Jude 24). When we let our friends know that we have hope and confidence in them, we are following the example of Jesus and of Scripture.

Involvement

Motivation for change also comes from involvement. Charles H. Kraft in his excellent book *Communicating the Gospel God's Way* observes that there are three approaches to communication—or, for our purposes, disciplemaking. There is the monolog/lecture method (*ugh!*), the dialog/discussion method (*better!*) and the method of life involvement (*best*). What Kraft is saying is that the best way to influence others to be disciples of Jesus is to be involved with them personally, to share your total life, to be a role model, to be a friend.

Jeff and Laura were disciplemakers who took this very seriously when they discipled Ann, a nineteen-year-old waitress. Ann was on her own for the first time when Laura and Jeff met her at a local restaurant. As they got to know Ann, they discovered that all was not well with her. She was out of money and needed a place to stay. They invited her in. She left eighteen months later, a Christian and ready to be a leader in a local InterVarsity group.

During those eighteen months, Jeff and Laura shared their lives with Ann. They went shopping together. They went camping. They spent many hours in discussion. Jeff and Laura talked about

Jesus openly, though Ann made it clear, at first, that she was not interested in religion.

Even though Ann was not interested in religion, she did want the quality of life Jeff and Laura had. She saw their struggles, fears and joys. She watched them relate to their neighbors. She saw their relationship with each other.

As Ann watched, Jeff and Laura prayed. Their persistence paid off. One night Ann came home depressed after a rough day at work. She began to ask questions about Jeff and Laura's faith in God and how anyone could actually believe in him. Five hours of discussion later, Ann became a new creation.

In the weeks following, Jeff and Laura cared for and nurtured this new person. They read the Bible with her regularly. They went to church together and sometimes had their own worship services at home. After each day at work, they talked about their experiences. They counseled Ann as she began to date young men from church. She grew to know and to serve Jesus.

Involvement, of course, has many forms. Not everyone is gifted for live-in involvement as Jeff and Laura were. Jesus was intimately involved with twelve and less intimately involved with hundreds of others. For some, involvement does mean inviting the Anns of our lives to live with us. For others, involvement is less intense. I do a lot of discipling over cups of coffee in the local MacDonald's. My involvement often takes the form of responsive listening. I get involved in the issues of my friends' lives and consider various biblical options with them. I have a friend whose disciplemaking efforts focus on meeting practical needs of those she hopes will follow Jesus. Others may disciple by working with younger friends to correct social injustices.

The important thing is not that my involvement look like anyone else's involvement. It is rather that our lives become intertwined with a few other people whom we can help be disciples of Jesus. Involvement means I give of my time, my skills and my love. It means, again, following the example of Jesus, who became a human being in order to become involved with us.

Information

Finally, motivation for change comes from information. Change seldom happens in a vacuum. When one person sees something in another's life that he would like to emulate, he needs information in order to change. He needs to know how the person he admires lives out his convictions. Here again, the initiative must be ours. When I was a young Christian, I assumed that my life alone would witness to Jesus' lordship. Then I overheard a friend say about me, "I always knew she was different, but I never knew why." I had never offered her the information she needed for the change she was ready to make.

As we offer information necessary for change to take place, we need to remember what the learning theories confirm: one person learns information in one way, and another in a very different way. I once complained to someone that the only place I ever got any good teaching was from books. I thought this was a reflection of the poor Christian teaching available to me at the time. I've since decided that it was a reflection of the fact that I receive information best in written form. In fact, it was a book, given to me by someone who loved me, that first convinced me to turn to Jesus.

So if we intend to influence people to change, to give them direction for their faith, then we need to discover and to respect the best way they learn or receive information. It may be in written form, through listening, in pictures or diagrams, or by doing.

For some, a picture is worth a thousand words. For others, a thousand words may communicate more.

Jesus, as we might guess, was a master at teaching people in the ways they could learn best. With the Pharisees, Jesus emphasized the written law (see Mk 7:5-13). Peter, in Acts 10, needed a vision to see how God wanted him to change, but in another situation, Jesus saw that Peter needed an activity (fishing) in order to learn (Lk 5:1-10). With people who learned by listening and talking, Jesus asked questions (Mk 8:17-21). Jesus did not teach all people in the same way, nor did he always use the same style with any individual. He saw their needs and he reached out to help them in the way that he knew they could receive it best.

In your own disciplemaking efforts, be sure to avoid imposing your favorite ways of receiving information on your friends. Try to be creative in presenting information about biblical truths. For some, you may want to emphasize reading. Another may learn more by going to a movie with you and discussing it afterward. Another may learn best on the tennis court.

Don't make the mistake of limiting your influence to your own learning style. (If I did that, only bookworms would become disciples through my efforts!) Instead, think of ways to use your friends' strengths. I think of Brad, a student who persistently "forgot" to read the assigned Bible passage before he met with his friend, Ron, for Bible study. Rather than fight Brad's distaste for reading, Ron asked him to read the passage aloud at the beginning of each study. Since Brad learned best by listening, reading out loud was an effective way to get the Word of God into him.

I am also reminded of Joe, a student who grew up on a farm. He learned to drive a tractor by driving a tractor, not by reading the manual or by watching someone else drive. So I decided he would learn best by doing, and I put him in charge of a student committee to plan the fall conference. He modeled it, not after my carefully planned outlines, but after another conference he had attended. The conference was a success, Joe's self-esteem skyrocketed, and he returned to campus with a renewed confidence that he could work out his faith in daily life.

What we have been saying about change dovetails with a cardinal principle of disciplemaking: Our goal is not to reproduce ourselves or prepackaged Christians, but to help our friends become all that Jesus wants them to be. We look at our friends with the hope and confidence that they can grow. We get involved with their lives to do all that we can to facilitate that growth. And we give them information, in the form they receive it best, to help them experience Christian maturity. All the while we stand beside them, looking at Jesus, the master at helping people change.

Notes
[1]Madeleine L'Engle, *Walking on Water* (Wheaton, Ill.: Harold Shaw Publishers, 1980), p. 122.
[2]Milton Mayeroff, *On Caring* (New York: Harper & Row, 1971), p. 44.

Putting It All Together
1. Think of one past experience where you learned something new. What was it?
What helped you in the learning process?
Now think of one time recently where you made an important change in your life. What was it?
What helped you make that change?
What do you observe from these experiences about how you learn?
2. When was there a time when you resisted change?
Why didn't you want to change?
3. When has someone helped you . . .
by offering hope?
by getting involved with your need?
by giving you information?
4. Take the learning styles test at the end of the chapter. What learning style are you?
What examples of this can you think of from your life?
Think about Jesus' ministry as recorded in the Gospels. List three

times when he taught people and the different approaches that he used.

Resources for Helping People Change

Resource 1: Ways of Learning
As you seek to influence your friends, to teach them and to see them learn and grow, it may help you to be aware of at least one common theory of learning. This theory divides learners into the main categories:

1. *Visual learners*—people who learn best from the written word, pictures and diagrams.

2. *Auditory learners*—people who learn best by listening.

3. *Touch-movement learners*—people who learn best by doing, by practical involvement.

What kind of a learner are you? What kind of a learner is the one you want to disciple? It will be important to consider these questions as you work at disciplemaking.

The test on p. 136 may help you discover your learning style. It was reprinted from Paul Welter's in *How to Help a Friend*.[1] Put a check beside any and all descriptions which are true of you. Go to the chart now, and then return to this page for evaluation.

After you have completed the chart, you are ready to evaluate. Add up the number of checks in each column. Whichever column had the most checks is probably your strongest learning channel. It could be that you have an almost equal number of checks in more than one column. This just means that you have more than one strong learning style.

Notes
[1] Paul Welter, *How to Help a Friend* (Wheaton, Ill.: Tyndale House, 1978), p. 191.

Checklist for Discovering Learning Channels

I. Strong in Visual Channel

___ 1. Likes to keep written records
___ 2. Typically reads billboards while driving or riding
___ 3. Puts model together correctly using written directions
___ 4. Follows written recipes easily
___ 5. Reviews for a test by writing a summary
___ 6. Expresses self best by writing
___ 7. Writes on napkins in a restaurant
___ 8. Can put a bicycle together from a mailorder house using only the written directions provided
___ 9. Commits a Zip Code to memory by writing it
___ 10 Uses visual images to remember names
___ 11. A "bookworm"
___ 12. Writes a note to compliment a friend
___ 13. Plans the upcoming week by making a list
___ 14. Prefers written directions from employer
___ 15. Prefers to get a map and find own way in a strange city
___ 16. Prefers reading/ writing game like "Scrabble"

II. Strong in Auditory Channel

___ 1. Prefers to have someone else read instructions when putting a model together
___ 2. Reviews for a test by reading notes aloud or by talking with others
___ 3. Expresses self best by talking
___ 4. Talks aloud when working a math problem
___ 5. Prefers listening to a cassette over reading the same material
___ 6. Commits Zip Code to memory by saying it
___ 7. Uses rhyming words to remember names
___ 8. Calls on the telephone to compliment a friend
___ 9. Plans the upcoming week by talking it through with someone
___ 10. Talks to self
___ 11. Prefers oral directions from employer
___ 12. Likes to stop at a service station for directions in a strange city
___ 13. Prefers talking/ listening games
___ 14. Keeps up on news by listening to the radio
___ 15. Able to concentrate deeply on what another person is saying
___ 16. Uses "free" time for talking with others

III. Strong in Touch/ Movement Channel

___ 1. Likes to build things
___ 2. Uses sense of touch to put a model together
___ 3. Can distinguish items by touch when blindfolded
___ 4. Learns touch system rapidly in typing
___ 5. Gestures are a very important part of communication
___ 6. Moves with music
___ 7. Doodles and draws on any available paper
___ 8. An "out-of-doors" person
___ 9. Likes to express self through painting or dance
___ 10. Moves easily; well coordinated
___ 11. Spends a large amount of time on crafts and handwork
___ 12. Likes to feel texture of drapes and furniture
___ 13. Prefers movement games to games where one just sits (this may also be a function of age)
___ 14. Finds it fairly easy to "keep fit" physically
___ 15. One of the fastest in a group to learn a new physical skill
___ 16. Uses "free" time for physical activities

Resource 2: Discipling Activities for Various Learning Styles
Once you know your learning style and the style of the friend you
are discipling, you will want to pick activities that enhance learning for your friend's particular style. Obviously, there are endless
creative options. The list of suggestions below is intended to
stimulate your thinking so that you can come up with ideas that
will be helpful to both you and your friend.

Activities for the Visual Learner
   Discuss articles
   Read books, poetry or music lyrics
   Do inductive Bible study
   Study Jesus' parables
   See and discuss movies
   Discuss photos and articles in photographic magazines
The following books are ones that would appeal especially to the
visual learner. Try discussing them from a biblical standpoint.
   The Way of the Wolf (The Gospel in New Images), by Martin Bell,
   Seabury Press, NY, 1968.
   Ragman and Other Cries of Faith, by Walter Wangerin, Jr.,
   Harper and Row, 1984.
   The Book of the Dun Cow, by Walter Wangerin, Harper and
   Row, 1978.
   Dark Horse, by John Fisher, Multnomah Press, 1983.
   The Little Prince, by Antoine de Saint Exupery, Harcourt, Brace,
   and World, Inc., 1943.
   The Velveteen Rabbit, by Margery Williams, Avon Books, 1975.
   Novels by Madeleine L'Engle (*A Wrinkle in Time, Journey with
   Jonah* and others).

Activities for the Auditory Learner
   Listen to tapes
   Discuss music lyrics

Discuss a movie
Discuss personal issues in light of biblical teaching
Attend and discuss lectures, workshops

Activities for the Touch-movement Learner
Take your student of evangelism along to help you present the
gospel to a seeking person
Put the person in charge of a project that will involve mastering
some new skills
Plan and go on a trip together
Make decisions together
Do simulated exercises (these are group activities involving the
reenactment of an event in order to explore the truth or prin-
ciples of the event. See *Using Biblical Simulations,* by Miller,
Snyder and Neff, Judson Press, 1973.)
Use your imagination! Perhaps a game of charades of real-life
happenings, followed by discussion, could help your friend
grow.

12

HOW TO USE SCRIPTURE IN DISCIPLEMAKING

Most people know who Miss Scarlet is. At least most people who are under fifty and grew up in the United States. She is, of course, one of the heroines of the famous game Clue.

Larry was a Clue fan, but he wasn't so sure about doing Bible study. When I first met him, he was a brand-new Christian, unsure of his faith and unskilled in reading Scripture. He liked to throw out difficult questions, aiming particularly at his Christian roommate, Bob.

Bob had told me about Larry. In fact, the whole InterVarsity chapter had prayed that Larry would become a Christian. God had answered that prayer, but Larry was still in the spiritual delivery room. When I came on the scene, I asked him if he would like to investigate some of his questions in light of Jesus' teaching in the Gospels. We became detectives, looking for clues, not about Miss Scarlet or Professor Plum, but about how Jesus would deal with Larry's questions.

I learned right along with him. We challenged each other each week to act on what we had just seen in the passage studied. He couldn't believe that there was so much material relevant to his own personal struggles.

One study came from a question he had about his parents. He was angry with his father, angry enough never to see him again. But he was willing to see what Scripture had to say about it. We looked together at Matthew 10:21-35 (the parable of the unmerciful servant). As we studied Jesus' words, "[Forgive] not seven times, but seventy-seven times," Larry began to cry.

"But how?" he asked. "I just don't have the strength."

It was not easy for him. It was at least a month before he was ready to begin a new relationship with his father. But the power of the Holy Spirit was at work in his life to change his attitude about his parents. It took him years to develop a strong relationship with them. But that passage and others that we studied gave him strength and hope that he could begin again.

Larry became convinced that the Bible is powerful, relevant and life-changing. I saw Larry's own life and attitudes change before my eyes.

The Power of Scripture

I have not always seen Scripture as life-changing. When I became a Christian, I began to memorize Scripture and read it regularly. But I didn't think of Scripture as actually being alive or being God's Word. I watched other Christians discuss the Bible and try to live their lives by its teaching. But at first I didn't connect what I saw with the power of Scripture. Then I realized that the people

I respected were growing primarily because they studied the Bible and applied it to their own lives. I decided that there must be something very special about that book.

About that time an InterVarsity conference speaker helped me see snow in a different way. What he said changed my view of Scripture.

It had snowed on the Saturday morning of the conference. The speaker reminded us of the snow covering the ground outside. Great ammunition for a snowball fight, he said. Fun to ski on. Lots of work to shovel. Beautiful and peaceful. But the most amazing thing about snow is that it brings life. As it melts, rivers flow, reservoirs are filled, the water table rises, and flowers bloom. Then the speaker reminded us that this is what the Word of God does also. "As the rain and the snow come down from heaven, and do not return to it without watering the earth and making it bud and flourish, so that it yields seed for the sower and bread for the eater, *so is my word*" (Is 55:10-11, emphasis mine).

God's Word gives life. It causes growth. It is the primary way God helps Christians change. It is itself living and active. It penetrates our thoughts and attitudes (Heb 4:12). It has power over sin (Ps 119:11). It has power to give strength when we are weak (Ps 119:28). Helping someone learn to find this life, this power, is one of the most important parts of disciplemaking.

Jesus knew how important Scripture would be in the lives of his followers. "Everyone who hears these *words of mine*," he said, "and puts them into practice is like a wise man who built his house on the rock. . . . It did not fall, because it had its foundation on the rock. But everyone who hears these *words of mine* and does not put them into practice is like a foolish man who built his house on sand. The rains came . . . and it fell with a great crash" (Mt 7:24-27, emphasis mine).

Jesus' words are serious business. People do not like their houses to fall down. In Denver there is a residential area built on clay. Many of the houses have cracked foundations. Needless to say, real estate does not move quickly in that area.

When we help young Christians study Scripture, we are helping them build spiritual houses which can weather many storms. Moses wrote to the Israelites, "These commandments that I give you today are to be upon your hearts. Impress them on your children. Talk about them when you sit at home and when you walk along the road, when you lie down and when you get up. Tie them as symbols on your hands and bind them on your foreheads. Write them on the doorframes of your houses and on your gates" (Deut 6:6-9). Paul wrote to Timothy, urging him to continue living according to the "Holy Scriptures" which Timothy had known from infancy. Paul reminded him, "All Scripture is God-breathed and is useful for teaching, rebuking, correcting and training in righteousness, so that the man of God may be thoroughly equipped for every good work" (2 Tim 3:16-17).

It is interacting with Scripture more than anything else which equips a young disciple to grow. When my friend Brent became a Christian, someone advised him to become "saturated with Scripture." Brent took that advice very seriously. He read the Bible. He learned how to study the Bible on his own. He listened to teaching based on Scripture. Most of all, he tried to live out the truth of Scripture in his life. Personally, I am glad he did, because my own life has been influenced by his love of Scripture. He has become a teacher of Scripture. His model of a godly husband and father is a constant reminder to me of the value of Scripture in living out our faith. His model makes me want to be saturated with Scripture too.

Interacting with Scripture in a way that saturates our lives can take place in many settings. It can happen in church as the pastor teaches. It can happen in small Bible-discussion groups. It can happen as a casual comment is passed on from friend to friend. Hopefully, those you disciple will learn God's Word in all these settings. But let me give you five specific suggestions for what you can do in your discipling relationships to help your friends meet God in the Bible: *emphasize discoveries, list influential passages, emphasize biblical stories, address your friend's needs* and *be patient.*

Emphasize Discoveries

Educators tell us that people learn best when they discover an idea on their own. This is true in Bible study as well as in other areas of life.

I had the experience of interacting with an older Christian for a period of several weeks. During that time I made several very significant and very personal discoveries about my walk with God. Later, I heard my mentor speaking to a large group of people. He gave them a list of observations which he thought were critical to understanding the Christian life. Every one of his points was one of "my" discoveries! I had not known that he was teaching them to me.

The gift my mentor gave to me was to let me discover these things on my own. They are my truths now. Years later, I am still influenced by them. If he had just told me the "answers," I'm certain I would have forgotten them by now.

The method of Bible study which best allows for discovery is the *inductive method* or, if you will, the detective method. It is the approach to Scripture which looks at what it says and then tries to solve life's mysteries by the truths available.

First, *observe.* What are the facts you know from the passage?

Next, *interpret.* What do these facts mean? What does this mean about the nature of God? of man? of life?

Then *apply.* What does God want me to be or to do, right now, in light of this passage?

Develop the skill of asking questions naturally. This is especially important when there are only two of you in the study. When you're in these relationships, try to be a comrade-in-arms with your friends, discovering truth together. You are not the authority, the expert. Scripture is. You are, furthermore, modeling for your friends what to do when questions arise and you are not around. Your friends can look for clues to solve the mysteries of life independently. This is much more valuable to them than a list of ready-made answers, which may or may not prove helpful in their own situations.

You can use this approach to Scripture without any extra textbooks. But if you find you want a tool to guide you, you might want to purchase *Leading Bible Discussions* (IVP), a short, helpful instruction book. Another suggestion is the LifeGuide Bible study series (IVP), which will give you many good questions in a number of books of Scripture and on a number of topics. Also, the resource section following this chapter has more Bible-study ideas.

List Influential Passages
Another suggestion for using Scripture in disciplemaking is to develop a working list of Scripture passages that have influenced your life. You can use passages you have studied in your own devotions, heard about in a sermon or read about in a book. Your list can be topical or by Scripture reference. They should be passages that you are excited about because they have influenced your life. If you have not been moved by the text, you are probably not the one to present it to a friend.

When I asked Ray to lead a Bible study in our church, he definitely was not interested. Then as I began to share my excitement about a passage I had just studied myself, he began to reconsider his reluctance. Eventually, he led a study on that same passage.

Emphasize Biblical Stories
Emphasize stories in Scripture, especially at the beginning. We

live in a visually oriented society. Most people under thirty grew up watching television (as well as playing Clue!). We are accustomed to seeing and relating to stories and pictures. Stories help us to think and process the message.

But this was nothing new to Jesus. He continually used stories and metaphors throughout his ministry. He knew what would capture people's attention. We need to be as wise. Our Bible studies should include many real-life stories, either from character studies actually in the Bible, or from the applications we can make of biblical truth to our daily lives. Along with your list of Scripture topics, you might want to develop a working list of character studies and real-life dramas described in Scripture. Also, be sure to check out the many Bible-study guides in the bibliography on page 205.

Address Your Friends' Needs
Find out what your friends' interests and questions are. You may love eschatology and want to study Revelation. Your friends may want to learn how to pray or how to date or how to live with their roommates. Tailor-make your Bible studies to fit your friends needs. (Again, see the resource section at the end of this chapter.) Develop a short-term plan for Bible study, about six weeks long. The discipling process takes much longer, of course, but your plan at this point should be short. Be flexible. The important thing is for young Christians to see that the Bible speaks to their daily needs and that studying Scripture can really change who they are and how they respond to life's struggles.

Be Patient
Don't push your friends to grow too fast. Have patience.

I have struggled with this in my relationship with Karen. When she began coming to our Bible study, I thought she was a Christian. She seemed especially sensitive to Scripture and anxious to apply it to her life. She was open in the group and with me. Yet slowly it became apparent that Karen did not know Jesus. And when this became clear to her, she was eager to meet him. Her conversion was dramatic and exciting for both of us.

But it didn't turn out the way I had hoped. Karen is growing much too slowly for me. She has never established a quiet time. She struggles with consistency in her walk with God. She chose not to go to a weekend seminar that would have helped her in so many ways. I felt it was important that she attend. But she did not seem to be concerned. Though she cannot share the story of her conversion without tears, it seems to go no further.

I was shocked at my response: anger, impatience and hurt. My expectations were not being met. I was helpless. And I came to the conclusion that all I could do was pray. Even as I am still praying, rather than talking, suggesting or persuading, I continue to struggle with why her growth seems so minimal over these six years. I am trying to turn over the responsibility for results in her life to God. Maybe Karen is growing in different ways than I expected. Or maybe God sees her growing when I cannot. I have asked him to deal with my impatience, pride and lack of compassion.

When I am impatient for growth, both in myself and in my friends, I remember the words of a Scottish hymn writer of the last century, Horatius Bonar:

> The Creator, in the silent majesty of power, noiseless yet resistless, achieves by a word the infinite wonder of omnipotence! In order to loose the bands of winter . . . He does not send forth His angels to hew in pieces the thickened ice, or to strip off from the mountain's side the gathered snows, or to plant anew over the face of the bleak earth, flowers fresh from His creating hand. No! He breathes from his lips a mild warmth into the frozen air; and forthwith, in stillness, but in irresistible power, the work proceeds.[1]

So it is God's work from the beginning to the end. He began by speaking his Word. Now he uses his Word to bring about growth. He has given us his Spirit which breathes life into those who hear his Word. And he has given us the grace to work beside him, loving, teaching and supporting the young Christians in our lives.

Putting It All Together
1. Describe the first time you remember ever studying the Bible.
2. List the times in the last month when you were exposed to Scripture (sermons, personal devotions, Bible studies, books or otherwise).
Which times were most helpful to you? Why?
3. In an average week, how much time do you spend interacting with Scripture?
4. Do a short Bible study on John 1:1-7, using the A-B-C plan described in Resource 1 at the end of this chapter.
5. Think about your learning style. (See chapter ten.) What effect does your learning style have on the way you study the Bible?
What learning style is most difficult for you to relate to in Bible study?
Why?
6. When have you seen Scripture change your life?

Resources on Using Scripture in Disciplemaking

Resource 1: The A-B-C Plan of Bible Study
Don Fields, InterVarsity staff member in Indiana, suggests to those he disciples that they use the A-B-C plan when they look at a passage of Scripture.

A—*Analyze* Put the passage into your own words. What are the facts stated in the passage? Express these in terms common today.

B—*Best verse* Choose it and memorize it.

C—*Contract* Find a command to obey, a promise to claim or a principle to practice. Write down what you intend to do to obey what God is telling you in this passage of Scripture. Be very specific.

Don says:

If God spoke to you about loving the people on your dorm floor, don't pray, "Lord, help me to love everyone on my dorm floor." Say, "Lord, remind me to pick up my clothes because my roommate is a meticulous person and my sloppiness bugs him." Or, "Lord, remind me to turn down the stereo when my roommate is studying because he can't concentrate. . . . Lord, remind me to turn the lights off at a reasonable hour when my roommate is trying to sleep."

When you get this specific, you are involved. We should not say, "I should," "I ought," "I must," but, "by your grace I will."[1]

When you suggest the A-B-C plan of Bible study to your friend, you might also suggest that you both work on the same passage a few times and compare notes. This plan will help you both be very specific about what God is teaching you. You can expect to see your lives being changed by Scripture.

Notes

[1] I copied down this quote from Horatius Bonar many years ago and no longer know its source.

[2] Don Fields, "How to Take Hold of the Bible," *HIS* magazine 30, no. 4 (January 1970): p. 23.

Resource 2: One-on-One Bible Studies: Partners in Discipleship

You may prefer to use more structured Bible-study material than the A-B-C plan just described. In that case, there are innumerable guides on the market. Many are excellent. I have listed some in the bibliography, beginning on page 205.

The following Bible studies may interest you immediately. They were originally published as *Partners in Discipleship,* by Dan R. Kirkbride, published in booklet form by InterVarsity Press. We've reproduced them here for you to use in your discipling relationships.

Week One
You've Only Just Begun

Study: Moses and Joshua
The Israelites' forty-year desert trek is almost over as they defeat their last opponent before crossing the Jordan River. Read Deuteronomy 3, and imagine Moses as a wise, old general reviewing and encouraging his troops.
1. Why does Moses remind Joshua of the victories over the enemy kings of Bashan and Heshbon?
2. Write down an incident from your history in which you won an important battle. What part did God play in the victory?
3. What is the significance of Moses' past disobedience?
4. What have been the lasting effects of disobedience in your life or in the world?
5. In verses 23-28 Moses recounts his visit with God. What messages does he have for Joshua now? for the future?
6. Who has God put in your life to help you maintain your perspective on history and the future? Pause now to pray, thanking God for that person. Where may you be able to go that he or she never could?
7. God may lead you to be another person's mentor as he led Moses to be Joshua's. What are some ways you could "charge, . . . encourage and strengthen" that person?
8. Why do we not need to be afraid when God places a difficult task before us?
9. Summarize the passage's teaching about God. Rejoice through prayer that he has only begun to show his greatness to you.

Central truth: If we consider God's steady hand in history and that he fights our battles, we will not balk when he asks for even greater obedience.

Further reading on Moses and Joshua: Exodus 17:8-16; 24:12-18 and Numbers 13:1—14:38.

Activity: *Getting to Know One Another*

Purpose: To review your personal histories and lay the groundword for future involvement.

Spend at least forty-five minutes together, perhaps over a cup of coffee or an ice-cream cone. Taking a cue from Moses and Joshua, each take fifteen minutes to review your spiritual histories with one another. Also discuss hobbies, special interests, future plans, birthdays, school and family.

Conclude your conversation with prayer, thanking God for the unique person your partner is and for the prospects of friendship and discipleship.

Week Two
The Lord's Loyal Love

Study: *Jonathan & David*

King Saul brought David to his court (1 Sam 18) but soon grew jealous of him. Saul's son Jonathan, however, loved David very much. He was willing to help David escape if his father tried to harm David. The episode concludes with a covenant, a pact reaffirmed several times in Jonathan and David's years together.

1. Read 1 Samuel 20:12-17. What are Jonathan's responsibilities in his agreement with David? What are David's?

2. What are specific ways you could demonstrate "the loyal love of the LORD" (v. 14) to a close friend?

3. Name a formal agreement you have made and fulfilled. (It could be a promise, contract, vow or membership agreement.) How did the agreement itself help you fulfill your responsibilities?

4. After Jonathan's death David honors his memory in a lament: "Jonathan lies slain on your heights. I grieve for you, Jonathan, my brother; you were very dear to me. Your love for me was wonderful, more wonderful than that of women" (2 Sam 1:25b-26). What does this passage suggest about how the two men carried out the vows described in 1 Samuel 20?

5. How would these men's lives have been different without one another's friendship? What difference did God make in their relationship? In the weeks to come, be alert for God's work in your life through your partner.

6. Complete the activity before concluding.

Central truth: God's loyal love, active in all facets of our lives, is a model for human interaction.

Further reading on Jonathan and David: 1 Samuel 18:1—20:11; 23:15-18 and 2 Samuel 9.

Activity: Covenanting the Future

Purpose: To specify your expectations for your time together.

Jonathan initiated a covenant with David which both men honored. Take the remaining time to write down your commitment to one another. It should be a covenant detailing several aspects of your relationship.

Mutually agree on the covenant's terms. Make it livable. Here is a sample:

We agree to the following expectations for our one-to-one partnership.

Study times and location: Tuesdays from 1 to 2 P.M. in the Old Union.

Meeting dates: We will meet for our study on October 9, 16, 23, 30, and November 6 and 13. Our midweek project times will be established at each study.

Punctuality: Meetings will begin and end at agreed times.

Intercessory prayer: We will pray for each other's personal growth and needs at least every other day, utilizing a prayer list.

Quiet time: To keep ourselves spiritually fit we will have a personal quiet time (Bible study and prayer) at least twenty minutes per day, five days per week.

Expiration date: This covenant expires at 2 P.M., November 13, 19XX.

Date: October 2, 19XX

Signed: _____ & _____

Week Three
We Live If You Stand

Study: Paul & Timothy

The second letter to Timothy is Paul's last letter and perhaps his final communication to Timothy. He recalls what they have shared: "You, however, know all about my teaching, my way of life, my purpose, faith, patience, love, endurance, persecutions, sufferings . . ." (3:10-11). 1 Thessalonians 3:6-13 recounts one of these shared experiences. Timothy has just returned to Corinth with a report on the Thessalonian church. As you study, consider how this incident contributed to Timothy's understanding of Paul.

1. Read 1 Thessalonians 3:6-13. What is Paul and his company's situation when Timothy arrives with his report? How does it change after the report?

2. What does Paul do in response to the report?

3. Paul is not simply glad that the Thessalonians' faith is healthy; their faithfulness is vital to his life (v. 8). Who is an older Christian whose life may be encouraged and strengthened to see you "standing fast" in the Lord?

4. If there is anyone you have helped become established in

Christ, how do you react to news of the person's spiritual well-being?

5. In what ways does Paul hope to see God work in the Thessalonian church? Why can Paul trust God so boldly?

6. Which of the qualities in 2 Timothy 3:10-11 did Timothy observe in Paul's wholehearted dealing with this church?

7. How might you put some of these principles to work in caring for your partner in discipleship?

Central truth: Paul's active care for the Thessalonians included prayer, a desire to visit them and identification with their success and failure.

Further reading on Paul and Timothy: Acts 16:1—17:15; 19:1-22 and Philippians 2:19-24.

Activity: Sharing Extended Prayer

Purpose: To pray together for the needs in the world and for yourselves.

Paul demonstrated to Timothy an active prayer life and a willingness to live out his prayers. Follow his example, and set aside at least a half-hour to pray together. Thank God for what he has done, and petition him in two areas—for others and for yourselves.

Thank God for what he is doing in the world. Consider how he is relieving suffering and establishing his church. A current news magazine may help focus your requests for the world's needs. Pray for missionaries in the same ways you pray for yourselves for they share many of your needs. Intercede for government officials, farmers, doctors, your families or your local churches. The possibilities are endless.

Thank God for his grace in your lives and in your relationship with one another. Ask him not only for immediate needs but also for long-range answers. Pray for character qualities you would like to develop.

Some hints: Find a quiet, comfortable place; pray in short sentences to help your partner concentrate; and do not spend half your time talking about requests—pray.

Week Four
The Rookie's Friend

Study: Barnabas & Paul

The apostle Paul was not without a trainer. He was befriended by a man so encouraging that the apostles changed his name from Joseph to Barnabas (which means "son of encouragement").

Note the help Paul (at this time still called Saul) receives from Barnabas. It demonstrates how you can develop the potential of a partner in ministry.

1. Read Acts 9:26-31. Though several years have gone by since his conversion on the road to Damascus, Saul is making his first trip to Jerusalem. Why is he not accepted there?

2. On what basis does Barnabas defend Saul? Why is this risky to Barnabas's reputation? to the Christian community?

3. How can you faithfully stand up for a Christian whose character is questioned.?

4. What benefits came to the Christian community because they accepted Saul? (Note: Hellenists were Jews who had adopted some aspects of Greek culture. Paul himself was one.)

5. Saul remains in Tarsus for several years until a need for teaching arises in Antioch. Read Acts 11:19-26. Why do you think Barnabas particularly sought out Saul?

6. Imagine Barnabas's excitement as he explained to Saul God's activity at Antioch. For what can they praise God?

7. As Saul learned from Barnabas, what can your partner learn about God and about ministry from spending time with you?

Central truth: God used Barnabas's ability to see and encourage others' potential to nurture the early church.

Further reading on Barnabas and Paul: Acts 12:25—15:34-41.

Activity: Having Fun
Purpose: To have fun and discover new facets of one another's personalities.

Do you think Barnabas and Saul spent a whole year pastoring in Antioch without ever having fun? I doubt it. You two should also cut loose and plan a recreational outing. There is only one guideline: have one person pick one of his or her special interests. It need not necessarily be something you both love to do.

Why not a mutual decision? You will learn more about one another by sharing one another's passions. So whether it is attending a cello concert, swimming, visiting a photography darkroom or hiking, make sure it is one of the planner's favorite recreations. During Week Seven the other partner can choose an activity.

Week Five
A Son and the World Too

Study: Abraham & Isaac
Now you will meet a father-and-son pair. While Abraham and Sarah are still childless, God promises to make a great nation of their descendants. Finally, at age 100, Abraham fathers the promised son. When the boy is twenty-seven years old (according to historian Josephus), God gives a command to Abraham.
1. Read Genesis 22:1-19. What does God ask of Abraham?
2. Imagine the moods of the four travelers on their way to Moriah. What thoughts fill Abraham's mind during the three-day journey?
3. Do you think Abraham really equated sacrificing Isaac with worship (v. 5)? Explain.
4. Abraham offers his son—a classic example of trust in God. How would Isaac describe the experience to *his* sons?

5. What are you tempted to withhold from God? How might that prevent him from producing lasting works in your life?

6. How will Abraham's obedience profoundly affect the generations which follow him (vv. 15-18)? How might God work through obedience and your one-to-one relationship to bless future generations?

7. What does this passage teach about worship? Pray together that if God asks for difficult personal obedience, you will respond with faith and trust.

Central truth: If we withhold nothing from God, he will use our obedience to produce lasting works.

Activity: Visiting a New Friend

Purpose: To remind you that your relationship should reach out.

Plan to visit another person: an elderly person from your church, the woman who sits beside you in botany class, a newcomer on campus. The most important thing is to get out and do it. Introversion will destroy a one-to-one relationship.

You may show compassion, share the gospel or just be a friend. If you plan a scary encounter, take heart from Abraham's trusting in a difficult time. God honored his trust not only by returning Isaac but also by blessing all humanity through his active faith.

Remember to pray in weeks to come for the friend you visit.

Week Six
Nothing Is Impossible with God

Study: Elizabeth & Mary

Two famous mothers shared the experience surrounding their sons' births. Elizabeth tenderly reassured Mary at a difficult time in the young girl's life. Study Luke 1:5-56, aiming to become a person who can help a friend in a crisis.

1. What exciting news do Zechariah and Mary receive? Compare

their initial reactions.

2. Does Elizabeth react to her role as you would expect her to? Why or why not?

3. Imagine yourself as Mary. What fears come to mind?

4. How does God care for Mary through the angel's appearance? her kinship with Elizabeth? the timing of events?

5. What indicates that Elizabeth is a woman of strong faith? How does that make her a fit mother for a man like John? a likely encourager for Mary?

6. If you were Mary, what aspect of Elizabeth's character and works would you have found most encouraging? How does Mary's praise song (vv. 46-55) demonstrate that Elizabeth helped her believe?

7. As Elizabeth encouraged Mary, how could you encourage each other in the ministries God has given you?

8. Describe Elizabeth's day-to-day life with God which prepared her to minister as she did. Pray together for each other's discipline in developing such qualities.

9. Make plans for this week's activity before concluding.

Central truth: Because Elizabeth was spiritually strong, she was able to help Mary during a crisis.

Activity: Inviting Friends to the Study

Purpose: To introduce another pair to the idea of one-to-one relationships.

This session does not require a special meeting. Rather, take a few moments to think of another pair who might be suited to a one-to-one experience together.

Commit their future together to God in prayer. Invite them to the next study. Who knows? A new partnership may be formed.

Week Seven
Never Say, "Never"

Study: Jesus & Peter

Jesus walked with his disciples for three years, but his final evening with them was especially memorable. He not only taught them; he also served them. Read John 13:1-20, and see how this simple act redefined the meaning of leadership for one of the Twelve in particular—Peter.

1. In verses 1-11 Jesus twice alludes to information about himself and about the disciples which is yet to be revealed. What are the two mysteries?

2. What early statements by John demonstrate Jesus' strong sense of identity? How do you think this knowledge might have helped him be a foot washer?

3. On entering houses visitors usually had their feet washed by the lowest servant. Is there a job that you consider too low for you to do? How would you feel if called on to do it for Christ's sake?

4. According to Jesus, did everyone need a bath? a foot washing?

5. How can pride cause us to miss out on Jesus' (or one of his disciples') cleansing ministry in our lives? What loss do we risk if we refuse Jesus' work in our lives (v. 20)?

6. Jesus said that putting our knowledge about serving into action leads to blessing. Name a specific way you might minister to your partner. Does anything prevent you from doing it?

7. How might this incident redefine Peter's definition of leadership? How will your service be different for having spent time with your partner?

Central truth: Allow Jesus to minister in your life as he desires so that you may receive him and also the One who sent him.

Further reading on Jesus and Peter: Matthew 14:22-36; Mark 8:27—9:13 and John 21:1-23.

Activity: *Having Fun Revisited*

Purpose: To give the other partner a chance to shine.

This time the second partner plans a recreational activity. The same rule applies: one partner picks something he or she likes to do. It is always fun to discover new facets of people's character when they perform on their own turf. Also, allowing a person to shine in a specialty is another form of service.

While on this outing, casually review your weeks together. What went well? Which activity lacked punch? Was the covenant an effective tool? How could it have been made more effective? What innovations would you try in sharing this course with another partner?

Conclude your time with prayer. Thank God that he ministers to the whole person and has provided deepened friendship with your partner.

Week Eight
Give Me Two Scoops

Study: *Elijah & Elisha*

Elijah prophesied in the ninth century B.C. In 1 Kings 19:16-21 he calls an apprentice, Elisha. Their final day together represents the change of leadership inevitable in every Christian ministry. Identify with Elisha. Just as he "received the mantle," so will you too.

1. Read 2 Kings 2:1-22. What fact is revealed about Elijah's future? Name the parties that share this information.

2. What is the contrast between Elijah's wishes and Elisha's? Trace their travels on a map.

3. Is Elisha's request of the departing Elijah wise? Why or why not?

4. Think of an admired Christian peer or a more mature believer you know. Which of his or her qualities would you gladly accept?

5. What spiritual quality in your partner do you admire? What might keep you from emulating the qualities of another believer?
6. What are four ways that God confirms the transfer of Elijah's spirit to Elisha? (Note: Sons of prophets were members of prophetic guilds or schools. Both Elijah and Elisha once served as presidents of such groups.) Do you think Elisha is a good successor to Elijah? Why?
7. Why may a change from good leadership not necessarily be something to fear?
8. God may eventually guide you to leadership in your Christian circle. How has the time with your partner better prepared you to serve?
9. Consider together others who may be interested in becoming partners in discipleship. Pray for them.

Central truth: Stick faithfully to your Elijah that you may be ready when God calls you to lead.

Resource 3: How to Help Your Friend Have a Quiet Time

1. Give your friend a copy of *Quiet Time* (IVP) and plan a time to discuss it after the person has read it.
2. Share about the importance of time alone with God: God desires to be with us and to have our attention. Any relationship takes time and energy if that relationship is to grow. Jesus took time apart from others and received refreshment and direction from the Father.
3. Help your friend decide on a time and a place to have a daily time alone with God. Discuss the importance of regularity and faithfulness.
4. Give your friend a copy of the booklet *My Heart Christ's Home* (IVP), and discuss it.
5. Offer to meet with your friend for a certain number of times to demonstrate a quiet time.
6. Set up a system of accountability. For example, if your friend

has decided to have an early morning quiet time, but has difficulty getting out of bed, offer to take a cup of coffee to the
person's dorm room or to make a phone call to encourage the
person to get up.

7. Meet weekly for a few minutes to discuss what you are both
learning in your quiet times and how they are going. Discuss
integrating into life the principles and commands you are learning from Scripture.

8. Suggest Bible-study guides, materials and methods that will
help your friend get into Scripture. (InterVarsity Press's LifeGuide
Bible study series as well as *This Morning with God, Quiet Time
Companion* and *Search the Scriptures* are good helps.)

9. Share about the use of a hymnal to aid in worship and med-
itation.

10. Mention the value of a pen and notebook to write down
impressions, thoughts and ideas God is teaching.

11. Help your friend get started keeping a prayer list in a notebook. This is helpful not only in remembering what to pray for
but in seeing how God is answering prayer.

12. Discuss different types of prayer and how to integrate them
into prayer times: adoration, praise, thanksgiving, confession,
offering yourself to God for his service and petition. Start a list
of Scripture passages that demonstrate each type of prayer.

13. Share the importance of position when praying. For many
people, being on their knees can help them center on God and
be humble before him.

14. Spontaneously share what you are learning from Scripture.

15. Discuss the importance of allowing times of silence for listening to God. (You might be interested in reading *The Other Side
of Silence* by Morton Kelsey. This is a guide to Christian medi-
tation published by Paulist Press.)

16. Pray for your friend as the person endeavors to establish one
of the most important disciplines of life.

Resource 4: Topical Passages for Bible Study

The best way to come up with topical passages to use in your discipling relationship is to consider what passages have made a strong impression on you. Begin to compile a list of passages that have gripped you and that you can use enthusiastically.

In the meantime, here is a sample list of passages which have changed me. I use these in my own discipling relationships. Many are stories with a message. They may provide a place for you to start formulating your own list.

Quiet Time
Joshua 1:1-8
Psalm 1
Psalm 119:1-16

Evangelism
Mark 4:35-41
John 3:1-15
John 3:16
John 4:1-26
John 11:17-44
Ephesians 2:8-9

Jesus: Lord and God
Mark 2:1-11
John 1:1-5, 14
John 20:24-31
Philippians 2:5-11
Colossians 1:15-20
Hebrews 1:1-14
Revelation 20:11—21:6

God's Concern for the World
1 Kings 20:23-30
Isaiah 49:1-6
Acts 1:1-8
Acts 10

Forgiveness and Forgiving Others
Nehemiah 1
Psalm 51
Isaiah 6:1-8
Matthew 18:21-35

Guidance
Judges 7
Psalm 25
Psalm 32:8-11

The Holy Spirit: Who and What
John 14:15-20
John 16:5-15
Acts 2:1-4, 37-41
Romans 8:9

Consider becoming well acquainted with one book of the Bible to be able to use it effectively. I use the Gospel of Mark and I would encourage you to know a Gospel well. Developing a list will cost you—time and energy. But it is well worth it!

13
HOW TO HELP YOUR FRIEND SHARE THE FAITH

Once upon a time (this is a true story), a long time ago (when Joram was king of Israel), the city of Samaria didn't have enough food. In fact, the famine was so bad, some people resorted to cannibalism (2 Kings 6:28-29). In the city there were four men who had leprosy. One day they decided to venture into the enemy camp and see what was happening there. "We are going to die here," they reasoned, "so why not go to the enemy and surrender ourselves?"

When they arrived at the campsite of the enemy, they found it deserted. (They didn't know it, but God had scared all the people away.) They found food, jewels, silver and gold. After they ate as much as they wanted, they began to collect the loot from the camp. Suddenly, one of them remembered the folks back in their own city. "We're not doing right. This is a day of good news and we are keeping it to ourselves. . . . Let's go at once and report this to the royal palace" (v. 9). And so they went back and told their countrymen the good news.

For the original version of this story, see 2 Kings 7:3-17. For a modern-day application of this story, look at your own life and at the lives of those you are discipling.

Presumably, you have found spiritual and intellectual satisfaction, emotional healing and an ongoing sense of living life as it was meant to be, now and in eternity. Granted, we are all in process. Some days I am more excited about the good news than other days. But on *any* day, I dare not keep silent when I have an opportunity to tell a friend what I have found. I dare not "collect the loot" without telling others. My emotional, spiritual and intellectual growth may not be all I want it to be, but because God is at work in my life, I have good news to share.

This sharing of the good news is crucial to the disciplemaking process. God became man to share the good news. Angels sang to shepherds to share the good news. Jesus lived with his disciples to share the good news. And we live with our friends to share the good news.

Not everyone is called to be an evangelist. Evangelism is listed as one of the special gifts of the spirit (Eph 4:11). But everyone is called to be a witness (Acts 1:8). Paul wrote to the Corinthians that Christians are ambassadors for Christ (2 Cor 5:20). I like that designation. I can relate to the image of an ambassador. Ambassadors represent their country in other countries. They look out for the interests of their own country. They do their best to help people see the merits of their homeland. They never become a citizen of the countries in which they are living. They are polite about cultural differences, but they always maintain their national identity.

As disciples and as disciplemakers, we live in a foreign land. We represent Jesus to people who are not Christians. It makes sense, then, to look at Jesus' life and see how he lived in a foreign country. In fact, Jesus even said, "As the Father has sent me, I am sending you" (Jn 20:21). How, then, did Jesus live out his witness to the Father's love? What is there in Jesus' example that we should try to teach those we are discipling?

Jesus understood the people because he had become one of them. He served the people by meeting their practical needs. He taught the people. And he modeled a relationship with God the Father. We can look at each of these areas of Jesus' life to get ideas about how we can reach out to those who live around us.

Identifying on a Human Level

First of all, Jesus became one of the people he was serving. He became man even though he was God (Phil 2:6-8). Likewise, we need to identify with those who live in the country where we are ambassadors. This does not mean that we participate in the degrading effects of sin. Jesus never did that (Heb 4:15). Our identity with non-Christians occurs, not on a spiritual level, but on an emotional, human level. In fact, the more mature we become as Christians, the freer we are to identify with non-Christians. We are free to be honest with ourselves, because we know that God will not be shocked or withhold his love. To the extent we are honest with ourselves, we become more self-aware. And as we become more aware of our own needs and foibles, we can relate to others without fear or judgment.

I can understand the loneliness, frustration and boredom of my non-Christian friends. Jesus, as a man, knew what it was to be thirsty, tired and sad. I know what it is like to be parched spiritually, to be tired emotionally and to experience great sadness. So I can identify with non-Christian friends who feel that way. But I am not entirely like them, because I have also experienced

God's goodness in satisfying these needs.

Serving Those around Us

Jesus became like us in order to reach us, but he also served us in order to reach us. Similarly, as ambassadors for Jesus, we need to serve those around us. One of the people I know who does this well is a pastor in New England who virtually grew his church by ministering to the community. When he heard that a young high-school student in town had received serious burns from an accident, he regularly traveled a hundred miles to minister to the family and their son in the hospital. Before the accident my pastor friend had never met the family. Today they are part of his church.

The area of serving others is an excellent one for the disciple-maker to teach by modeling and by shared experiences. Look for opportunities to serve fellow students or your neighbors down the street. Then take your friend with you as you serve. It will be more fun, and your example will become a means of growth for your Christian friend.

Becoming Teachers

But Jesus taught with words as well as deeds. If we limit ourselves to our example, few will become Christians or grow in their faith. If we live our lives in the power of the Spirit and do not tell others how they can receive his power, then we may do more harm than good. It is our lives of love, understanding and service which draw people to the point where they are ready to hear words of instruction. Some people err in evangelism by giving answers to questions that have not been asked. Others err by never giving the answers. We need to help our young disciple friends learn to live their lives so that their friends will ask questions, and then we need to help them give the answers.

Becoming a Christian is a reorientation of life. It begins in a moment, but it lasts a lifetime. Jesus spent much of his time on earth teaching the disciples about the kingdom of God. A quick look at any red-letter edition of the New Testament shows how much information he gave them. As we disciple young believers we need to help them reorient their lives around kingdom values, and we need to study the teachings of Jesus with them so that they, in turn, will be able to teach others.

Modeling Relationship with God

Finally, Jesus modeled a love-relationship with God the Father. He allowed his disciples to see him pray (Mt 26:36-43). He talked about his relationship with the Father (Jn 14:28-31). He let them know that his own life was motivated by obedience to the Father (Jn 17:4). This kind of modeling can be part of our evangelism as well as our disciplemaking efforts. We can tell non-Christian friends that we will pray for them. We can let them know how God answered prayer for us or how he touched our lives recently. We can even share with them some of our own struggles to obey him. We can model the life of faith as well as teach it.

One of the greatest frustrations of learning to be an ambassador is that an ambassador's effectiveness is seldom measurable. In helping younger Christians learn to share their faith, we can't promise them one hundred per cent yield on the seeds they plant. (Not even seed companies do that!) But we can promise that God will be at work, nurturing each seed, influencing it and eventually giving fruit in season.

I have always been fascinated by the ability of seeds to germinate when they are many years old. One of my favorite stories was told by Ben Logan in *The Land Remembers*. He wrote:

During work on a railroad cut in Manchuria in 1926, some lotus seeds were found, buried deep under an old lake bed. Geologists said the seeds might easily be four hundred years old. The seeds were planted. They germinated, producing lotus plants of a type no one had ever seen in that area. Later, when carbon-14 dating came into use, those lotus seeds were tested. They were at least eight hundred years old . . . and they were still alive.[1]

When we plant seeds of faith, we need to remember that our God is timeless, the great I Am (Ex 3:14). Fruit which we do not see may be harvested years later. Not too long ago a friend told me about a conversation he had had with a nonbelieving acquaintance. The interesting thing was that they picked up on a spiritual topic that they had discussed when they knew each other twenty years earlier. The non-Christian man remembered in detail what his Christian friend had told him. He had been thinking about it for twenty years!

But God in his kindness usually does not make us wait that long to see the fruits of our work. I have heard story after story of people who have become Christians, been discipled by older Christians and then shared their faith so that others, in turn, became Christians.

The Fruits of Modeling

Let me tell you about someone whose life was changed because a group of students took seriously God's instruction to be ambassadors.

David was a student at a large Midwestern university. Three years ago, the InterVarsity chapter sponsored meetings on the campus mall and invited an evangelistic speaker to come for a week of meetings. In preparation for the event, the chapter held training sessions for the Christians on campus.

Lisa, a student in the chapter, went to these sessions not because she wanted to witness, but because she wanted to obey Jesus. She had become a Christian in high school and had been influenced and discipled by several older Christians. Her Christian friends had taught her that sharing the faith is not an optional part of Christian obedience. When the day came for the first evangelistic meeting, Lisa was there on the mall. She told me afterward that she was scared. She had been "trained" to witness, but her emotions had not gotten the message that her ears had heard. She looked around for someone standing alone. There was David, on the edge of the crowd. Lisa walked over and stood beside him. Finally, she got up enough nerve to say, "So, what do you think about what this guy is saying?"

What Lisa, in her fear, did not know was that God had been at work in David's life for months before the meeting. David was in fact fascinated by what "this guy was saying." And he was eager to talk more with Lisa. David came back to the other meetings on the mall that week, and Lisa invited him to the InterVarsity meeting on Friday night.

At the Friday night meeting Lisa introduced David to some of the men in the chapter. They befriended him and talked more David went back to the dorm and became a Christian.

His friends immediately helped him get involved in a discipling relationship with an older Christian student. Today, David is a leader in the campus fellowship. He is busy sharing his faith and helping younger Christians grow.

Lisa acted in obedience to Jesus even though she was scared. One of my best friends is a woman of similar conviction. I met Jennifer when she was already a mature Christian. One day I asked her to tell me about the beginnings of her faith. The story she told me was so moving that I asked her to write it down. Here is what she wrote:

I became a believer because Cynthia witnessed to me. But, quite frankly, Cynthia intimidated me. She was a resident assistant in my dorm and had an opinion about everything. I was a gum-chewing, political activist from the Bronx. Cynthia and I were opposites.

That's why Cynthia invited me to be in her Bible study. She

felt pressured to start an evangelistic Bible study, but she didn't want to. So, she invited the four people she thought would be the least likely to accept the invitation. That way she could say she tried, and be free of her obligation.

But all four of us said yes. I don't know why I agreed to come. My answer was out of my mouth before I knew it. "Sigh," I thought, "Now I'm stuck."

For four weeks, every Thursday evening, I trudged to Cynthia's room along with the three other women to study John's Gospel. I don't remember the studies. My impression was that I came (never missed one), talked and then left.

At the end of the four studies, I quit. I wasn't particularly touched or changed by them. Jesus was nice. The studies were fine, but mid-terms were coming. If Cynthia wanted to talk to me more about religion, she'd have to look for me in the smoking section of the library.

Two weeks after the study was over, there was a conference seventy-five miles away. I went with Cynthia because it was being held at an all-male college. I thought it would be a great place to meet men. Throughout the weekend I heard speakers and singing groups. It was "nice," but not life-changing. I was an observer.

I don't remember the last speaker's name. He began to preach from the Gospel of John. What a coincidence that it was the same passages we had talked about in Cynthia's Bible study. I stopped feeling impartial. I began to lean forward in my chair. He was speaking to me. I was caught up. Then he issued a call. I thought he was speaking directly to me. How could I ignore it? I stood up. Yes, I would follow Jesus. I had no other choice.

When I looked around, I saw standing next to me the three other women who had been in Cynthia's study with me. All of us had said yes to Jesus. All of us felt that we had no other option when Jesus called us to follow.

That was fifteen years ago. Today, all four of us are active Christians. In fact, we are all involved in some kind of full-time Christian service. I'm glad now that Cynthia reached out to me.

This is how God builds his kingdom. Cynthia and Lisa obeyed Jesus in spite of their fears. Jennifer and David are ambassadors for Jesus today because two students were obedient. As we obey Jesus' call to be disciplemakers, we too will be helping our friends learn to be ambassadors.

Notes
[1]Ben Logan, *The Land Remembers* (New York: Avon Books, 1975), p. 30.

Putting It All Together
1. Tell about the two or three people who had the most influence on your decision to become a Christian. How did each person influence you? What was most helpful to you as you came to the point of decision?
2. What experiences have you had in sharing your faith? What do you do best as an ambassador for Christ? What is the hardest thing for you about being an ambassador?
3. The author describes sharing the faith in terms of understanding others, serving others, teaching others and modeling for others. Can you think of instances in your own life or in the life of another person where you have seen these things lead to faith in Jesus?
    Understanding
    Serving
    Teaching
    Modeling
4. Read the story of the sower, the seeds and the soils in Mark 4:1-20. Which soil best represents your own life?

Think of a non-Christian friend. Which soil best represents that person's life?

What do you think is the best way to "work" that kind of soil?

5. What steps would you like to take in your own life in order to be a better ambassador?

Are you willing to ask two friends to pray with you about taking these steps?

Resources for Helping a Friend Share the Faith

Resource 1: Getting Started

1. Ask your friend how he or she feels about sharing his or her faith. What are their desires, fears and expectations? You might ask:

What thoughts and feelings do you have when you hear the words "sharing your faith"?

How was Christianity shared with you? What was positive for you? What was negative?

Tell me about your non-Christian friends.

What non-Christian friends are you actively praying for?

Which of them do you think might be open to the gospel?

How do you feel about sharing your faith with that person?

What might be some first steps you can take to begin?

2. After determining where your friend is in his or her thinking on this matter, decide on a book or two on evangelism that you might read and discuss (like *Out of the Saltshaker, How to Give Away Your Faith* or *Reinventing Evangelism*).

3. Study the Scriptures together to gain a biblical basis of evangelism. (See the LifeGuide Bible study *Evangelism.*) Look through the Gospels, and consider how Jesus related to people who needed to be drawn to himself. Discuss how these principles relate to your situations.

4. Pray together regularly both for the persons you are discipling,

for their needs and fears, as well as for their non-Christian friends. Share your own needs and prayer concerns for your non-Christian friends with whom you are sharing the gospel.

5. If your friend has no non-Christian friends, discuss building friendships and pray for non-Christian friends for them. Read chapter seven of this book together. Decide on a social activity you both enjoy, and invite one or two non-Christian friends to do it with you.

6. When your friend has established friendships with nonbelievers, talk and pray about the possibility of doing an evangelistic Bible study together. It should have a limited number of Christians in it and go for a limited time (six to eight weeks). See the books *How to Begin an Evangelistic Bible Study* and *Leading Bible Discussions.*

7. Model evangelism to your friend by inviting him or her along to spend time with you and your non-Christian friends. Or take him or her out and share an experience of contact evangelism: show him or her how to share Jesus with everyone you meet. (If you don't feel comfortable doing this alone, invite a mature Christian or a Christian leader to go along.)

8. Model and teach the essential part that prayer plays in evangelism. Stress the work and role of the Holy Spirit in bringing individuals to Jesus. (See *Evangelism and the Sovereignty of God.*)

Sample Plan C: Learning to Share the Faith   Discipleship Plan Worksheet: How do I grow in my faith?

Week/Date	Purpose	Activity Together	Reflection: Prayer requests? How did it go? What was learned?
1	1. Find out Linda's experience in evangelism. 2. Find out level of involvement with non-Christians.	Use questions from "Helping a Friend Start Sharing the Faith."	Linda has desire and good intentions but needs direction and accountability.
2	1. Provide motivation by example. 2. Pray for opportunities. 3. Present "Four-Week Evangelism Plan" (chapter 13 resource).	Read and discuss the testimony in "Helping a Friend Start Sharing the Faith." Pray together.	Linda seems hesitant but is willing to try the "Four-Week Evangelism Plan."
3	1. Ask how she is doing with evangelism plan. 2. Talk about difficulties. 3. Pray together.	Share progress in "Four-Week Evangelism Plan." Plan activity together with non-Christian friend. Pray.	**How is this person growing?** This is a critical time to pray that Linda will be encouraged.
4	1. Have fun. 2. Model interacting with non-Christian. 3. Ask good questions.	Go out for pizza with non-Christian friend.	**Evaluation of time so far. Any changes needed?** Linda seemed a little nervous but relaxed as evening went on. Pray for her friend.

Week/Date	Purpose	Activity Together	Reflection: Prayer requests? How did it go? What was learned?
5	1. Learn how to use media in evangelism. 2. Discuss how evangelism plan is going.	Attend movie. Critique what it is saying to our culture. Discuss how to use this with non-Christian friends. Review plan.	Linda is excited about sharing Christ with her friends!
6	1. Encourage next steps. 2. Praise God for what he is doing. 3. Plan another activity with non-Christian.	Discuss activities to do for evangelism. Share specific requests for non-Christian friends.	Keep praying.
7	1. Invite non-Christian friend to concert. 2. Model evangelistic conversational skills.	Attend Amy Grant concert with non-Christian friend. Have ice cream afterward. Discuss music, lyrics, etc.	**How is this person growing?** Linda's friend may be interested in a Bible study.
8	1. Evaluate. 2. Discuss next steps.	Review, share, evaluate experience. Pray; praise God. Ask Linda for feedback.	**Evaluation of last seven weeks: Where do we go from here?** May start evangelistic Bible study next month. Will phone weekly for accountability (Linda's idea).

Sample Book Study Schedule

Book _Out of the Saltshaker, Becky Pippert_

Date _____

Unit	Personal Preparation	Activities to Do Together
1	Read chapter 1.	Read Mt 28:16-20. What is Jesus' vision for the world? How does he want to accomplish it? Pray that you will have a vision for your world.
2	Read chapters 2 and 3.	Read Jn 4:1-30. How did Jesus build trust? Think of a non-Christian friend. How can you build trust with that person? Pray for that friend.
3	No reading.	Exercise: Find someone sitting alone on campus, and start a conversation about anything. Debrief over ice cream afterward.
4	Read chapters 4 and 5.	Study Jn 8:1-11. Describe Jesus' compassion and actions. How do you relate to the sins of those around you? Pray for non-Christian friends.
5	Review "First Steps to God" (see p. 175).	Exercise: Role-play telling the gospel to each other. Mark areas on which you need to work. Go to a movie with a non-Christian friend.
6	Read chapters 6 and 7.	Have a meal together. Talk about your changing feelings and observations about evangelism. Pray together.
7	Read chapter 8.	Exercise: Start a conversation with someone this week, and ask, "Are you interested in spiritual things?" Debrief afterward. Pray together.
8	Read chapters 9 and 10.	Study Lk 10:25-37. What are the characteristics of a good "neighbor"? How does this relate to evangelism? Pray together.
9	Read chapters 11 and 12.	Visit the student union or another campus gathering spot. Ask several students if they would like to talk about spiritual issues. Debrief.
10	No reading.	Study Acts 17:16-34. What is the heart of the gospel? Write down three intentions you have as a result of these ten weeks together. Pray together.

Resource 2: A Four-Week Plan for Developing Evangelism Skills
The following is a four-week plan to help your friends (and you)
learn to "get out of the saltshaker and into the world." It is adapt-
ed from *A 30-Day Evangelism Plan*, by Len Andyshak. His un-
abridged plan in the Pathfinder pamphlet series published by
InterVarsity Press. As you do these activities you may want to
create a chart as a checklist.

1. Start each day with a simple, specific prayer something like
this: "Here I am, Lord. Please heal me, strengthen me, introduce
me to the people you want me to love, and please give me opportunities to share with them about you. Amen." Check this off
on a daily chart (on page 182) as a reminder.
2. Read a book on evangelism. Set a goal for just a few pages a
day. (Five to eight pages is realistic.) You might choose *Tell the
Truth*, by Will Metzger (IVP), or *Out of the Saltshaker*, by Rebecca
Pippert (IVP). Check off this daily reading on the chart.
3. Introduce yourself to fifteen to twenty new people. This can
be done anywhere or any way your heart desires (the way the
Lord leads in answer to that prayer you prayed). Perhaps sitting
by someone in class and saying hello and getting the person's
name. Perhaps at a meal, at the hallway, running, in the store.
Who knows what the Lord may do? Record the names of the
people you meet on the chart, and review them daily so you don't
forget them. Forgetting is a deadly handicap in evangelism!
4. Four times during the month (once a week), spend some time
hanging around with a non-Christian friend or acquaintance. It
could be the same person each time or four different people.
Possibly it will be someone from those fifteen to twenty people
you've been meeting. This is to be a casual, nonreligious activity
of some kind—sharing a Coke or a cup of coffee, dropping into
the person's place to visit, going to a movie or a party, studying
together, jogging together, doing whatever sounds good to you.

Record what you did on your chart.

5. Four other times, invite one of your non-Christian friends to a church-related activity. The person doesn't have to accept. You just have to initiate. The invitation could be to church, a Bible study, a movie, a fellowship meeting, an evangelistic dorm talk, a potluck. You could even be daring and invite the person to look at Jesus in the Bible with you for a few weeks. Record this on your chart as usual.

6. Four more times in the month, simply ask a person about Jesus. You might start by asking, "What church did you grow up in? Are you still involved?" Then move to the question of Jesus: "What are your impressions of Jesus?" These questions will get you to the heart of the matter easily and quickly. You'll find people surprisingly open with you, especially after having established even a brief friendship with you before this point. As always, the key is to be sensitive to the Lord's guidance—the right person (perhaps not the one you expected), at the right time (perhaps at an inconvenient time or when you think you're not ready). Remember that simple prayer—he will indeed hear and he will indeed answer. You can expect some miraculous opportunities and wisdom from above in that moment. " 'Not by might nor by power, but by my Spirit,' says the LORD" (Zech 4:6).

7. At the end of the four weeks, choose one to three specific goals to continue your evangelistic momentum in the immediate future. Here is a list of several exciting and varied possibilities to choose from. If you are exceedingly wild, like Ezekiel or Jesus, you may be led to do something not even included in this list!

Meet at least two people per week at a meal.

Join your campus literature ministry.

Start an evangelistic Bible study.

Ask friends to read your testimony and give you feedback.

Write letters to non-Christian friends. Talk about your faith.

Ask non-Christian friends what they believe about Jesus.

Spend some time each week with a non-Christian friend.

Volunteer as a conversant in an English-as-a-second-language program.

Become friends with an international student.

Invite a non-Christian friend to some religious activity once a month.

Memorize the gospel outline.

Study part of the gospel in depth.

Study answers to questions often asked in evangelism.

Give a non-Christian friend a Christian pamphlet and ask for an opinion.

"Adopt" an elderly person, or visit a nursing home regularly.

Become a Big Brother or Big Sister.

Join a club to meet non-Christians with interests like yours.

Start or join an evangelistic drama or music group.

Keep praying that simple, gutsy prayer each day. Pray daily for a non-Christian friend—for specific steps toward the person's salvation.

Go through this program again.

Sample Four-Week Evangelism Plan

Week	Pray	Read	People	Casual Time	Discussion about Jesus
I	✓	pp. ——	——	——	——
II	✓	pp. ——	——	——	——
III	✓	pp. ——	——	——	——
IV	✓	pp. ——	——	——	——

Resource 3: Films and Media in Evangelism

The media today is a proven communicator. Contemporary ideas and philosophies are heard through it—many of which are contrary to the Christian faith. But the media can provide an excellent catalyst for discussion in a one-to-one or group setting.

Below is a set of questions you can use to discuss the underlying values of a media piece. After viewing a movie together, ask:

a. What Christian values are affirmed in the movie?

b. Where in Scripture are these values illustrated or discussed?

c. Make a list of other values that are communicated in this movie.

d. What answers from the movie do you find for the following questions?

What is reality?

Who is man/woman?

What happens at death?

What is the basis of morality?

What is the meaning of human history?

e. What image of Christianity is projected?

f. What is the basic world view of this media piece?

g. Can this be considered a Christian work? Why or why not?

Examples of Media Pieces to Use

Movies

Chariots of Fire—deals with Christian and secular values.

Cry Freedom/Do the Right Thing—deal with social-justice issues and racism.

Dead Poets Society—deals with purpose and motivation in life, individualism versus conformity and authority issues.

Field of Dreams—deals with the nature of faith and risk, and of reconciliation.

The Karate Kid—deals with how to teach or disciple.

Tender Mercies—deals with questions of pain.

The Mission—deals with the persecution of Christians.

Places in the Heart—deals with social justice, poverty, death.

Television

"60 Minutes" (CBS)

"Nightline" (ABC)

"48 Hours" (CBS)

Watch for special productions which might lend themselves to the questions above.

How to Obtain Media

Video rental store near you.

Videotape show from television.

Attend a movie theater.

Purchase a copy of the movie.

Resource 4: First Steps to God: An Evangelistic Tool

If your friends want to share their faith, but aren't sure what to say, you can do two things to help them. First of all, help them write out their own experience of coming to Jesus. This will help clarify in their own minds what they will say when someone asks them how they became Christians.

Then you can suggest that your friends memorize the following "First Steps to God." This is a summary of the gospel. This summary has been used effectively for many years to help people understand what it means to have faith in Jesus Christ.

God

God loves you (Jn 3:16).

God is holy and just. He punishes all evil and expels it from his presence (Rom 1:18).

Man

God, who created everything, made us for himself and expects us to find our purpose in fellowship with him (Col 1:16).

But we rebelled and turned away from God (Is 53:6). The result is separation from God (Is 59:2). The penalty is eternal death (Rom 6:23).

Christ

God became a human being in the person of Jesus Christ to restore the broken fellowship (Col 1:19-20a). Christ lived a perfect life (1 Pet 2:22).

Christ died as a substitute for us by paying the death penalty for our rebellion (Rom 5:8). He arose and is alive today to give us a new life of fellowship with God, now and forever (1 Cor 15:3-4; Jn 10:10).

Response

I must repent for my rebellion (Mt 4:17).

I must believe Christ died to provide forgiveness and a new life of fellowship with God (Jn 1:12).

I must receive Christ as my Savior and Lord with the intent to obey him. I do this in prayer by inviting him into my life (Rev 3:20).

Postscript

As I completed editing this book, I was drawn to reread Paul's letter to the young man he discipled. Did I remember his advice? Did this book follow it? I discovered that the old truths of Scripture are always new truths when I apply them afresh. This time the "new truth" involved pots. . . .

Pretend you are a vessel, a pot. Would you rather be a flowerpot, a chamber pot or a soup tureen? Would you rather be made of clay or of sterling silver? Would you rather be used for serving food to company or for carrying out the garbage?

Some of us might choose to be flowerpots and some of us would rather be soup tureens. But I'm sure we would all agree on the other options! God's Word says that we are, in fact, like vessels. And that we have a choice about how we are to be used.

In a large house there are articles not only of gold and silver, but also of wood and clay; some are for noble purposes and some for ignoble. If a man cleanses himself from the latter, he will be an instrument for noble purposes, made holy, useful to the Master and prepared to do any good work. (2 Tim 2:20-21)

I've struggled in the past with those verses about the vessels. I grew up in a democratic society where everyone is supposedly equal. I don't like someone telling me that some Christians (pots) are used for "noble" purposes and some for "ignoble" purposes. But that's what the Bible says.

This time as I read about the pots, I saw that we have a choice. Our usage is not imposed on us by a careless despot. When we choose to cleanse ourselves from ignoble things, from values and activities that are inferior and base, then we will be used for noble purposes, for purposes of the highest value. Disciplemaking is certainly a noble purpose. I'd like to think disciplemakers may be silver serving trays in the kingdom of God.

I was reminded to try to live a holy life in order to be a noble pot. I was reminded to "flee the evil desires of youth [desires which are usually self-centered and of temporary value] and pursue righteousness, faith, love and peace" (2 Tim 2:22).

This time through Timothy's timeless letter I was also reminded of how much God loves me. I saw that even pots for noble purposes are put to hard use. Pots don't cry, but people do. And Paul wrote to Timothy that he prayed for him because Timothy had cried with him (2 Tim 1:4). I wonder what Timothy cried about. Because he struggled with sin? because he was so young? because he longed for people to know his Savior? I have cried for all these reasons. Paul's comfort to Timothy reminded me that God loves me.

Then I noticed Paul's other instructions to Timothy:

Fan into flame the gift of God, which is in you. (2 Tim 1:6)

Be strong in the grace that is in Christ Jesus. (2 Tim 2:1)

Endure hardship. (2 Tim 2:3)

Don't have anything to do with foolish and stupid arguments.
(2 Tim 2:23)

Watch your life and doctrine closely. (1 Tim 4:16)

Preach the Word; be prepared; . . . correct, rebuke and encourage. (2 Tim 4:2)

Is God telling me to do these things too? I think he is. I have seen
evidence in my life that God wants me to be a disciplemaker. God
wants me to do many of the same things he wanted Timothy to
do.

I am often scared, often foolish, often proud. I'm really not sure
why God gave me the job. And I still have lots of questions about
it. But "beyond all question, the mystery of godliness is great" (1
Tim 3:16). If I knew all the answers, the mystery would diminish,
and with it, the greatness.

We have a great calling. After all is said and done, disciplemaking is a great job. When I see a young Christian turn his heart
to Jesus, when I see God speak his Word through me, and when
I see him speak his Word to me, I stand in awe. God says to me,
as he says to all of us:

Pursue righteousness, godliness, faith, love, endurance and
gentleness. Fight the good fight of the faith. (1 Tim 6:11-12)

And we respond:

To him be honor and might forever. Amen. (1 Tim 6:16)

APPENDIX 1:
LISA AND LINDSAY:
AN INTERVIEW

Scientists know that what happens in the laboratory may be useless unless it can be reproduced and proven effective in the real world. Even if the stories in a book are true (as they are in this book), they were chosen because they were germane to the ideas the authors wanted to teach. In this way, a book is a sterile environment, something like a laboratory.

So I wanted to hear about a discipling relationship that is current, going on right now. With this in mind, I interviewed Lisa Adamovich, of Claremont, California, and the woman she is discipling, Lindsay Collins. I asked them to tell me how they got started and to talk about what they were learning. Every discipling relationship is as unique as the people involved, but Lisa's and Lindsay's experiences provide a framework for understanding the theories of disciplemaking which this book is all about.

Lisa, tell me about how you became a Christian and about how you got into the business of disciplemaking.

Lisa: I grew up going to church and believed in God since I was very young. In fifth grade I heard about Jesus from my Sunday-school teacher and became very interested in him. After my brother gave his life to Christ, I saw great changes in him and was drawn to Jesus. I was in the eighth grade then. I began to believe that Jesus was alive and at work changing people's lives. I was involved in my church high-school group and caught a vision for being part of a fellowship group.

When I went to college, I experienced profound growth through the InterVarsity chapter on campus. Tom Pratt, my staff worker, influenced me toward Jesus in some very significant ways—spending time with me, serving me, modeling radical commitment to God and passing on to me a deep love for Scripture, as well as some foundational tools for ministry. Because I had experienced God's love and power through the Christian community on campus and because I discovered that I had a real passion for ministry to students, I decided to join IVCF staff after graduation.

How did you meet Lindsay, and how did you first get the idea of pursuing a discipling relationship?

Lisa: I met Lindsay at a retreat at Catalina Island. I met and talked with many students, but I got the idea of pursuing Lindsay because I saw her great desire to grow spiritually and her openness to me personally. As I took steps toward the relationship, I saw God open up further opportunities. At one point Lindsay even asked me to disciple her.

Lindsay, how would you describe yourself when you first met Lisa? Tell us some of your first impressions of her?

Lindsay: When Lisa and I met at Catalina, I was eager to grow and to minister, but I wasn't very clear about what that looked like. But I thought I really had it together.

I really liked Lisa and was excited that she was going to be our staff worker in the fall. She was easy to talk to, and she seemed really interested in students.

So how did your discipling relationship get started?

Lindsay: When I came back to school in the fall, I began talking to Lisa about my summer mission in Hong Kong. She'd stop by or take me out. A few months later, I told her I'd like to live with her for the summer and continue being discipled. That's the first time we used the word to describe our relationship.

Lisa, what were your impressions of how you got started?

Lisa: I talked with Lindsay at Catalina and saw that she was a teachable, eager person, with a lot of gifts. I enjoyed her personally, and in the fall I began visiting her in her room. I asked her to do things, to pray with me and just to talk. I shared some of my vision and enthusiasm for ministry. I sensed God was leading me into a deeper relationship with her and was certain of this when she opened her life up to me further by asking to be discipled.

What did you "do" to disciple Lindsay?

Lisa: I made myself available to her, prayed with her, did ministry with her and served others with her. I had her over to my house a lot. I did practical favors for her. We went on longer trips for fun and took blocks of days to pray together. We studied Scripture together and worked together in a missions training program. I listened to her, and I challenged her on things that I noticed in her life. We went to places on campus she had never been before. At one point we lived together, and I modeled things I hoped she would learn.

I feel strongly that time twice a week at a coffee shop will limit a discipling relationship because only a few things can be modeled in that context. It was also important to me to build trust with Lindsay. Trust is crucial to all relationships, but especially in discipling. I tried to do this by being available, listening, taking an interest in what she was concerned for, affirming her, being honest and challenging and serving her in practical ways. When we are discipling people, we are teaching them how to be Christian leaders, which means they must build their authority on service and the Word of God. These things were all-important to me in my relationship with Lindsay.

What was one of the best things you did in the relationship? What fears did you have when you started? What were some mistakes you made or things you would have done differently?

Lisa: I think one of the most important things is to choose the right person, to choose someone who is genuinely interested in spiritual growth and is willing to act on Jesus' Word. Lindsay showed signs of being faithful, available and teachable. And I could see real evidence in her life of responses and decisions made which benefited her growth.

At first, I was more excited than afraid of the relationship. I saw such great potential. As the relationship developed, I feared raising certain issues and opening up areas of conflict. I feared my own lack of wisdom, and I feared that Lindsay would come to depend on me rather than on God.

As to things I'd do differently, I think I would have guided her first relationship with another young Christian more carefully to avoid unhealthy dynamics of dependency.

I have made a number of other mistakes, but God has really taken them and used them for good.

Lindsay, what were your expectations during this time? What were your fears? What has Lisa done in the relationship which has been most helpful?

Lindsay: I expected to be listened to and that Lisa would have godly and wise things to say. I don't remember having any fears, except that I might not be able to continue to spend as much time with her.

Lisa has imparted to me a vision, and she has let me in on

her discerning process so that I could learn to be discerning in ministry.

How have you changed during the time you have been in the discipling relationship with Lisa?

Lindsay: I've matured and deepened a lot. My responses to Jesus are much more real, solid and meaningful. I have clearer vision and discernment, and a growing ability to handle conflict. My passion has been given direction.

How has your relationship with Lisa affected your relationship with your fellow students? Have you been involved in discipling others? Could you describe some of those relationships?

Lindsay: My relationship with Lisa has caused some separation with those who don't have the vision for campus ministry that I have received from her. But it also helped many relationships become more healthy. I am an easier person to be with because of the ways I've matured.

I discipled one woman last year who grew a lot. I spent a lot of time with her, as Lisa did with me. But my friend and I became too dependent, and God had to cut us apart. I'm discipling a freshman woman this year, and that relationship is going well.

Lisa, what have been the benefits for you personally in the relationship with Lindsay?

Lisa: In Lindsay, I have a wonderful friend and partner in ministry. I have become a wiser and more loving person through our relationship. I have stretched myself in relationships, and it has made me a freer person. I have learned more about prayer. And it has given me a lot of joy to see a friend I have discipled growing in Jesus.

Lisa, what are some of your own conclusions about disciplemaking?

Lisa: In challenging others to disciple and in doing it myself, it seems we want some guaranteed, easy method. But actually, disciplemaking is risky. You may invest in a person's life for a few

years and then see them move away from God. It also costs a lot
to love people and involves suffering, especially in truth-telling.
It means valuing the person's growth more than her liking you
or affirming you. There is not a concrete method of discipling.
Jesus shows us some solid principles, but discipling is basically
relational, not programmatic. And it takes a long time. Spiritual
growth comes slowly. But I've concluded that it is well worth it.

Appendix 2
Sample Book Study Schedule

Book *Disciplemakers' Handbook*, Fryling et al.

Date _____

Unit	Personal Preparation	Activities to do Together
1	Read the preface and chapter 1.	Discuss together how you each became Christians. Study Mt 28:16-20. What do you think the disciples felt when Jesus said these words? How do you respond to them?
2	Read chapter 2, and write a summary statement.	List six words which describe God's relationship with the human race. List six words which describe your relationship with your friends. Discuss the similarities and differences.
3	Read chapters 3 and 4. What questions do you have about disciplemaking?	Together answer the questions at the end of chapters 3 and 4.
4	Read chapters 5 and 6.	Discuss your campus, neighborhood or work environment. What are the greatest barriers to intentional disciplemaking in your life now? Agree to pray together daily (this week) for overcoming these barriers.
5	Read chapter 7.	Each person invite a friend to dinner (together or separately). Make it a point to ask your friend two or three good questions. Afterward, discuss what happened.
6	Read chapters 8 and 9.	Interview three Christian friends. What or who influenced them the most to grow as Christians. Memorize 2 Tim. 2:2.
7	Read chapter 10.	Discuss with a pastor, counselor or IVCF staff member the most common emotional problems of your particular social group. Ask for ideas on helping those in pain.
8	Read chapter 11.	Take the learning styles test at end of this chapter. Find someone who learns in different ways from you. Compare what helps you learn and grow.
9	Read chapters 12 and 13.	Start a list of Scripture passages by summarizing three passages which helped you this last month. Make arrangements to read and discuss with a friend one book about evangelism.
10	Read the postscript and appendixes.	List three things you think God wants you to do as a result of reading this book. Ask at least two close friends to pray with you about these steps of faith.

APPENDIX 3: WHAT IF I RUN INTO TROUBLE?

Question: The person I am meeting with showed initial interest and agreed to a plan, but he has not kept our first two meetings. What do I do?

Answer: Be very candid. Ask if your friend really is interested. Perhaps unavoidable problems came up, or perhaps your friend just forgot. But it is also possible that he isn't willing to make the sacrifices necessary to grow as a disciple. If he indicates that he really does want to get together, ask if he'd like you to give him a phone call to remind him on the day before you are to meet.

Question: We started out strong, meeting weekly and growing, but after about four weeks things began to change. The woman I'm discipling missed a couple of times, came late or came unprepared. Is something wrong? Why the change?

Answer: There could be several reasons why this happened. You will need to ask your friend to find out the real reason.

If she is a student, there may be typical time pressures at exam time. Or it could be that God has used you to touch a sensitive growth point in her life, and she is struggling with it. Or perhaps she is realizing for the first time that there is a cost to growing as a Christian, and she may be unsure that she wants to pay the price.

It is important that you seek to bring the real problem out in the open. Then encourage and affirm what you see God doing in your friend's life. Be understanding and accepting rather than critical or judgmental.

You may need to release this person from the commitment of meeting together. But if you find you need to do this, it will be important for you to continue to befriend, encourage and pray for her. Trust God's work in her life, and anticipate the time when you can renew your discipling relationship.

Question: What if the person I'm discipling asks questions that I can't answer?

Answer: Relax! You are not an expert. You too are a learner, a growing disciple. Admit that you don't know the answer but you want to work with your friend to find it. Seek out an IVCF staff person, your pastor or a book for help and resources. (See the bibliography of this book for several key books you may want to purchase to have on hand in the future.)

Question: We have good times of sharing together when we meet, but we never seem to get to Bible study or prayer. Is this wrong?

Answer: You have an excellent foundation to build on. If you have agreed that Bible study and prayer should be part of your times together, then you will need to set some limits on your sharing. A kitchen timer may help. As you study and pray together, you will find your sharing becomes even more significant. It will flow out of what God is saying to you through his Word.

Question: We have been meeting together for about two months. Do we just keep meeting indefinitely?

Answer: It is important to set a limit on the number of times you will meet *before* you begin meeting. Then you will not be caught wondering how long to go on. When you come to your last agreed meeting, use it as a time to evaluate and praise God for what he has done. Then consider whether or not you are both willing to recommit yourself for another set period of time. You may end up meeting together for six months, but you will have more confidence if you do this in two-month chunks and evaluate regularly.

Question: What if the person I want to disciple says no to my proposal to meet together?

Answer: Trust that God is directing you and your friend. It could be that your suggestion was so new that your friend was not ready. But now that you've planted the idea, God's Spirit may create a readiness in the person for a future opportunity. (You might also talk to one of your close friends to make sure you are not presenting the idea in an offensive way.)

Question: As I spend time meeting with my friend, I'm discovering that she has a lot of doubt about God. What do I do?

Answer: Don't be afraid of this doubt. Accept your friend, and let her express her concerns. Doubt can be a very healthy catalyst for deeper spiritual growth. Commit yourself to help your friend address her doubt. If appropriate, seek out the support of a pastor or IVCF staff person.

Question: We've been meeting regularly but we are not as far along in the material as we planned. Is this okay?

Answer: Since your plan was intended to be person-centered rather than program-centered, you should be moving along at the pace that is best for your friend. There is no one perfect way to disciple someone. Relax and enjoy the pace that is best for both of you.

Question: Do we have to follow our plan each and every time we get together?

Answer: Not at all. Again, your focus should be person-centered, not plan- or program-centered. Be free to enjoy times of spontaneity and flexibility. These often become very special times, times of making memories.

Question: What if I need more help?

Answer: It will be helpful to you to seek out an older Christian who has had experience in discipling others as a resource person. Your pastor or IVCF staff person might be available to help. Or you might be able to correspond with someone who does not necessarily live near you but who could support you and pray for you in your efforts at discipling.

APPENDIX 4
INTER-VARSITY'S
SEVEN MINISTRY VALUES

The purpose of InterVarsity Christian Fellowship is to train college students to be godly men and women (or, for our purposes, to *disciple* men and women on college campuses). The following seven ministry values of IVCF can serve as a summary of our goal as disciplemakers. These seven values describe who we want to be and who we want those we disciple to become.

The vision of InterVarsity/USA is to build collegiate fellowships which engage their colleges in all of its ethnic diversity with the gospel of Jesus Christ and develop disciples who embody these biblical values:

1. *Evangelism* We believe that every person ought to have an opportunity to respond to Jesus Christ as Lord and Savior and to accept his invitation to follow him into a life of Christian discipleship.

2. *Spiritual Formation* We will teach and practice spiritual discipline (i.e., personal Bible study, prayer, reliance upon the Holy Spirit, worship) so that men and women can learn to grow in Christian obedience and Christlike maturity.

3. *The Church* We will serve the church by helping each person to appreciate its purpose and by encouraging their activity as lifelong worshipers and participating members.

4. *Human Relationships* We will teach and demonstrate by example the command of Christ that we love one another and that healthy human relationships are a mark of true discipleship and eventuate in fruitful friendships, marriages and working partnerships.

5. *Righteousness* Aware of the reality of evil as it exists in the human heart and in the social structures and systems of the global community, we will teach and demonstrate repentance and humility and the importance of personal integrity, compassion and prophetic renunciation and confrontation.

6. *Vocational Stewardship* We will challenge Christians to acknowledge the stewardship of personal skills and vocational opportunity so as to bring honor to God through our work in the college community, in the home or in the marketplace.

7. *World Evangelization* Believing that God has called all Christians to involvement in world evangelization, we will seek to help each person know how to hear that call and discover their place of maximum participation.

Bibliography

The following books are just a few to help you as you become a disciplemaker. The list is divided into categories, but since the topics overlap, you will do well to peruse the whole list.

The Christian Faith

Gill, David, *The Opening of the Christian Mind* (Downers Grove, Ill.: InterVarsity Press, 1989). Discussion of the importance of developing our minds as Christians living in a technological and pluralistic society.

Lewis, C. S., *Mere Christianity* (New York: Macmillan, 1964). A discussion of belief in God and following Jesus.

McCullough, Donald, *Waking from the American Dream* (Downers Grove, Ill.: InterVarsity Press, 1989). A comparison of our

American cultural values and biblical teaching. A good book to discuss with a young Christian.

Peterson, Eugene, *A Long Obedience in the Same Direction* (Downers Grove, Ill.: InterVarsity Press, 1980). A look at Psalms 120-134, discussing such themes as worship, service, joy, work, community and blessing.

—————— , *Run with the Horses* (Downers Grove, Ill.: InterVarsity Press, 1983). Peterson reflects on the life of Jeremiah, challenging readers to live life today at its richest and fullest.

Stott, John R. W., *Basic Christianity* (Downers Grove, Ill.: InterVarsity Press, 1958). A clear and compelling statement on the content of the gospel.

Bible Studies

Kuhatschek, Jack, *Taking the Guesswork out of Applying the Bible* (Downers Grove, Ill.: InterVarsity Press, 1990). Clear, basic, practical approach to understanding the Bible in order to apply it to personal life.

Le Peau, Andrew and Phyllis, *Ephesians,* A LifeGuide Bible Study (Downers Grove, Ill.: InterVarsity Press, 1985). The focus of this guide on Ephesians is the theme of wholeness in a broken world. It is helpful in offering hope to those you are discipling who are hurting and broken.

Lum, Ada, *How to Begin an Evangelistic Bible Study* (Downers Grove, Ill.: InterVarsity Press, 1971). The author tells how Christians can initiate and lead evangelistic Bible studies with their non-Christian friends.

Nyquist, James, and Kuhatschek, Jack, *Leading Bible Discussions,* A LifeGuide Bible Study (Downers Grove, Ill.: InterVarsity Press, 1985). In this completely revised and expanded edition, the authors discuss such subjects as how to form a group, how to study the Bible and how to lead lively discussions.

Sterk, Andrea, and Scazzero, Peter, *Christian Character,* A Life-

Guide Bible Study (Downers Grove, Ill.: InterVarsity Press, 1985). Excellent for individual and one-to-one study on such topics as temptation, holiness, compassion and servanthood.

Biblical Manuscripts
Reprinted text of the Revised Standard Version of the Bible on double-spaced 8 1/2 x 11 paper. Useful for one-to-one or small-group study of Scripture. About three-fourths of the Bible is available. Write: InterVarsity Christian Fellowship, 1550 E. Elizabeth, Suite 11, Pasadena, CA 91104.

Evangelism
Coleman, Robert, *Master Plan of Evangelism* (Old Tappan, N.J.: Revell, 1978). A study of how Jesus trained his disciples.

Little, Paul, *How to Give Away Your Faith* (Downers Grove, Ill.: InterVarsity Press, rev. ed. 1988; 1966). A practical book with advice for realistic communication of the gospel.

_____ , *Know Why You Believe* (Downers Grove, Ill.: InterVarsity Press, rev. ed. 1988; 1960). Little shows how Christianity consistently addresses major problems: Is there a God? Do science and Scripture conflict? Why does God allow suffering and evil? Is Christianity relevant?

Packer, J. I., *Evangelism and the Sovereignty of God* (Downers Grove, Ill.: InterVarsity Press, 1961). Packer integrates divine election with a Christian's evangelistic duty.

Pippert, Rebecca, *Out of the Saltshaker* (Downers Grove, Ill.: InterVarsity Press, 1979). A classic text on evangelism and how to develop an evangelistic lifestyle.

_____ , and Seimans, Ruth, *Evangelism: A Way of Life*, A LifeGuide Bible Study (Downers Grove, Ill.: InterVarsity Press, 1986). This study covers such subjects as overcoming fear, getting people interested in the gospel and creatively communicating the gospel.

Yancey, Philip, *Disappointment with God* (Grand Rapids, Mich.: Zondervan, 1988). Speaks to the questions: Is God unfair? Is God silent? Is God hidden? Good to discuss with Christians and nonbelievers.

Discipleship

Basler, Michael, *Discipling One to One* (Downers Grove, Ill.: InterVarsity Press, 1986). A short discussion on how to begin discipling others.

Kraft, Charles H., *Communicating the Gospel God's Way* (Pasadena, Calif.: William Carey Library, 1985). A study of how people are motivated to change.

McGinnis, Alan L., *Bringing out the Best in People* (Minneapolis, Minn.: Augsburg, 1985). A discussion of how to motivate people to learn.

White, John, *The Cost of Commitment* (Downers Grove, Ill.: InterVarsity Press, 1979). Discussion of the cost of being a disciple of Jesus Christ. Good book to use when beginning a discipling relationship.

Christian Living

Crabb, Larry, *Inside Out* (Colorado Springs, Colo.: NavPress, 1988). A book dealing with the problems of emotional and psychological pain in the Christian experience.

Grow Your Christian Life (Downers Grove, Ill.: InterVarsity Press, 1972). This book directs personal Bible study on topics such as personal evangelism, sin, growth, knowing God's will and marriage. It is designed for a daily twenty-five-minute study time.

Hyde, Douglas, *Dedication & Leadership* (Notre Dame, Ind.: University of Notre Dame Press, 1966). An ex-Communist party leader discusses how the church should go about training leaders.

Munger, Robert, *My Heart—Christ's Home* (Downers Grove, Ill.: InterVarsity Press, rev. ed. 1986; 1954). New believer adjusts to Jesus' coming to live in his heart.

Packer, J. I., *Knowing God* (Downers Grove, Ill.: InterVarsity Press, 1973). Discussion of the nature and character of God and how to get to know him.

Smedes, Lewis, *Forgive and Forget* (New York: Pocket Books, 1984). According to its cover, this book is about "healing the hurts we don't deserve." Another good book to discuss with a young Christian.

Quiet Time (Downers Grove, Ill.: InterVarsity Press, 1945). A classic book on practical methods for a meaningful quiet time. This book is a good starting point when trying to help someone establish a time alone with God.

Sittser, Jerry, *The Adventure* (Downers Grove, Ill.: InterVarsity Press, 1985). Exploration of the source, direction, barriers and power of discipleship.

Sterk, Andrea, and Scazzero, Peter, *Christian Disciplines,* A Life-Guide Bible Study (Downers Grove, Ill.: InterVarsity Press, 1986). This guide helps us to understand as well as practice spiritual disciplines such as prayer, Bible study, evangelism, worship and giving.

White, John, *Daring to Draw Near* (Downers Grove, Ill.: InterVarsity Press, 1977). A discussion of such people as Jesus, David and Daniel as they prayed.

——————, *Eros Defiled* (Downers Grove, Ill.: InterVarsity Press, 1977). White maintains compassion for the sinner struggling in areas of premarital and extramarital sex, homosexuality and masturbation.

——————. *The Fight* (Downers Grove, Ill.: InterVarsity Press, 1976). White looks at the basic areas of the Christian life: prayer, Bible study, evangelism, faith, fellowship, work and guidance.

Christian Love and Concern

Crabb, Larry, and Alexander, Dan, *Encouragement, the Key to Caring* (Grand Rapids, Mich.: Zondervan, 1984). Helpful advice on how to help friends in pain.

Huggett, Joyce, *Listening to Others* (Downers Grove, Ill.: InterVarsity Press, 1989). Instruction on how to listen effectively to friends in need.

Rohrer, Norman, and Sutherland, S. P., *Facing Anger* (Minneapolis, Minn.: Augsburg Publishing House, 1981). Practical advice for Christians trying to cope with their anger.

Shelly, Judith Ann, *Caring in Crisis* (Downers Grove, Ill.: InterVarsity Press, 1979). Six weeks of individual studies, with a group study for each week, to help Christians understand their responsibility to meet the needs of people in crisis.

Wilson, Earl, *Does God Really Love Me?* (Downers Grove, Ill.: InterVarsity Press, 1986). The author answers this question which Christians so frequently ask.

Worthington, Everett, *How to Help the Hurting* (Downers Grove, Ill.: InterVarsity Press, 1985). A discussion on how to counsel friends who have problems such as low self-esteem, poor self-control, loneliness, fear and depression.

For a catalog of good book ideas, write to InterVarsity Press, P.O. Box 1400, Downers Grove, IL 60515.

Videos

Consider joining with other friends, your church or IVCF chapter to rent or buy one of the following Christian videos:

Growing Closer featuring Gordon and Gail MacDonald. Building commitment in relationships, talking and listening, affirmation and rebuke, celebrating our sexuality and handling excess emotional baggage.

Out of the Saltshaker featuring Becky Pippert. Evangelism as a way of life, getting the story straight, learning to love and developing communication skills.

Give Me an Answer featuring Cliffe Knechtle. Has God spoken? Does God care for me? and Does Christian behavior discredit Christ?

These may be ordered from Twentyonehundred Productions, 6400 Schroeder Road, Madison WI 53707-7895. Write to this address for prices and more information on videos and audio cassettes available.